CHINESE CARVED LACQUER

CHINESE CARVED LACQUER

Derek Clifford

BAMBOO PUBLISHING, LONDON

First published 1992 by BAMBOO PUBLISHING LTD
8 Duke Street, St James's, London SW1Y 6BN

BRITISH LIBRARY CATALOGUING-IN-PUBLICATION DATA
A catalogue record for this book is available from the British Library.

ISBN 1 870076 20 6

Designed by Hugh Tisdale
Typeset by *wellSweep*
Printed and bound by Bookbuilders Hong Kong Ltd

ACKNOWLEDGEMENTS

Acknowledgements before a book like this are sometimes taken as a formal gesture, but only the author knows how much trouble he has caused to the keepers of public collections, to private owners, and to the experts of the trade during his researches. I am truly grateful to them all but particularly to those who waived or greatly reduced their charges and reproduction fees.

I am grateful to the Embassy of the People's Republic of China, the Embassy of the Republic of Korea, the Japanese Embassy, and the International Society for Educational Information in Tokyo for acting as effective middlemen between me and their national museums. Far Eastern museums that have permitted me to illustrate pieces in their collections are the Palace Museum in Beijing, the Shanghai Museum, the National Palace Museum in Taibei, the National Museum of Korea in Seoul, and the Tokyo National Museum. From Japan I have also been fortunate to have been allowed to illustrate two important pieces from the Engakuji Temple, Kamakura. In Britain I have been permitted to illustrate pieces from the British Museum, the Victoria and Albert Museum, the Fitzwilliam Museum, the Ashmolean Museum, the City of Aberdeen Museum, and the Percival David Foundation of Chinese Art. Continental European museums that have kindly allowed me to illustrate lacquer are the Linden-Museum in Stuttgart, the Museum für Ostasiatische Kunst in Berlin, the Museum für Ostasiatische Kunst in Köln, the Museum für Kunsthandwerk in Frankfurt am Main, the BASF Museum of Lacquer now in Munster, the Museum of Far Eastern Antiquities in Stockholm, the Rijksmuseum of Amsterdam, the Náprstekovo Museum of Prague, the Ráth György Museum in Budapest, and the Osterreiches Museum für angewandte Kunst in Vienna. Museums in the United States that have permitted reproduction of lacquer are the Asian Art Museum of San Francisco, the Los Angeles County Museum of Art, the Museum of Fine Arts in Boston, the Philadelphia Museum of Art, the Helen Foresman Spencer Museum of Art of the University of Kansas, the Freer Gallery of Art, the Arthur M. Sackler Gallery of the Smithsonian Institute, and the Cleveland Museum of Art. I have also most generously been given permission by Bluett & Sons Ltd., Sydney L. Moss Ltd., Spink & Sons Ltd., and Mr. Robert Peters to illustrate lacquer they have owned.

Other museums that have been of assistance are the National Museum of Denmark, the Art Institute of Chicago, the Philadelphia Museum of Art, the National Museum of Eastern Art in Rome, and the E. Chiossone Museum of Oriental Art in Genoa.

Additionally, I have been able to study the collections in the Musée Guimet and Musée d'Hennery in Paris, the Ferenc Hopp Museum in Budapest, the Hermitage Museum in Leningrad, the Metropolitan Museum in New York, the Brooklyn Museum, the Museum für Volkerkunde in Vienna, the City of Bristol Museum and Art Gallery, the Maidstone Museum, the Oriental Museum of the University of Durham, the Provincial Museum in Nanjing, the Provincial Museum in Xi'an, the Royal Scottish Museum of Edinburgh and Museum of Fine Arts in Boston.

To Dr. Hu Shih-chang of Hong Kong, Mr. Nicholas Harris, and Mrs. Desmond North I am grateful for permission to illustrate pieces in their possession. I am particularly grateful to the last who urged me to write this book when I was reluctant to do so, and has persisted in pressing me to complete it.

It is not possible to name all the individuals who have given me valued help, but I must particularly thank Mary Tregear of the Ashmolean Museum who initially pointed my enquiries in the right direction and Craig Clunas of the Victoria and Albert Museum whose understanding of the cultural background against which the art of lacquer flourished has been invaluable to me. He has generously shared his knowledge and saved me from several pitfalls; those which remain and into which I have fallen have been dug by my own obstinacy and ignorance. Finally, I am grateful to Clio Whittaker who has painstakingly sought out those irritating little errors to which authors are prone, to successive editors, Kym Ward and John Cayley, and to the book's designer, Hugh Tisdale, whom I have put under some strain.

CONTENTS

LIST OF PLATES

TABLE OF DYNASTIES

THE MAJOR DYNASTIES OF CHINA

Shang	*c.* 1600–1066 BC
Zhou	1066–256 BC
Han	206 BC–AD 220
Three Kingdoms	220–280
Jin	265–420
Northern & Southern Dynasties	420–581
Sui	581–618
Tang	618–907
Five Dynasties	907–960
Song	960–1279
Yuan	1279–1368
Ming	1368–1644
Qing	1644–1911
Republic	1912–1949
People's Republic	1949–

REIGN PERIODS OF THE MING & QING

MING DYNASTY	1368–1644
Hongwu	1368–1398
Jianwen	1399–1402
Yongle	1403–1424
Hongxi	1425
Xuande	1426–1435
Zhengtong	1436–1449
Jingtai	1450–1457
Tianshun	1457–1464
Chenghua	1465–1487
Hongzhi	1488–1505
Zhengde	1506–1521
Jiajing	1522–1566
Longqing	1567–1572
Wanli	1573–1619
Taichang	1620
Tianqi	1621–1627
Chongzhen	1628–1644
QING DYNASTY	1644–1911
Shunzhi	1644–1661
Kangxi	1622–1722
Yongzheng	1723–1735
Qianlong	1736–1795
Jiaqing	1796–1820
Daoguang	1821–1850
Xianfeng	1851–1861
Tongzhi	1862–1874
Guangxu	1875–1908
Xuantong	1909–1911

NOTE ON THE ROMANISATION OF CHINESE

The *pinyin* system of romanisation has been used throughout the text except in the case of quoted material, certain modern personal names and familiar 'postal' spellings (such as 'Yangtze', although the now familiar 'Beijing' for Peking has been substituted).

INTRODUCTION

This book is intended for the growing number of collectors and students who are interested in Chinese lacquer. The field is vast and to deal with all types in one volume would be likely to confuse, so this book concentrates on the most important group, that in which the decoration has been carved into a lacquer body. It traces the development of carved lacquer from its earliest certain appearance in the ninth century through to the tourist trophies manufactured in China today. Inevitably, the greatest attention has been given to the early and middle periods when most of the best work was done.

Particular care has been given to the selection of illustrations. Important datable pieces that are often only to be seen in small and unclear black-and-white photographs are here shown in colour. There is a considerable group from the Palace Museum, Beijing, which has not been widely illustrated in the West, and most of the rest are from lesser known museums and private collections and have not been published before. The plates are numbered and arranged sequentially and, like the book itself, follow a broad chronological progression. They have been distributed throughout the chapters and are designed to coincide with references in the text as far as possible. However, not all the illustrations are referred to explicitly and neither can all references to the plates come in neat sequence. The reader will occasionally be required to seek backwards or forwards in the book for a particular plate, and they are also asked to give some consideration to the captions of those plates for which there is no specific reference in the text.

Everyone familiar with the subject will be indebted to E. F. Strange, Fritz Low Beer, Sir Harry Garner, Sir John Figgess, Lee Yu-kuan ('Sammy' Lee), George Kuwayama, Klaus J. Brandt and others who have done much to clear the ground. Nevertheless newcomers with an enquiring mind will often want to know why pieces are said by these authorities to date from, say, the mid-fifteenth rather than the late sixteenth century, or more broadly why a piece is Qing rather than Ming. They will not be content to take a date on trust because Garner illustrated it as of a certain date, or because it appears in the National Palace Museum, Taiwan, attributed to such and such a reign. Maybe these attributions are right but blind faith is not for this eternally enquiring age. If there is a reason the enquirer will wish to know it, if there is only guesswork and hunch he should know that too. He may follow an authority by choice but not blindly.

Firm evidence for such an undertaking is sparse but we must make do with what there is. Controlled excavations give us limiting dates but during the carved lacquer centuries strangely little has been found in tombs so there is little information to be had from that source. After such certainties, or near-certainties, are set down there is still a lot left to do, great gaps of time left to fill and many pieces of lacquer for which to find a temporal home. If hearsay, tradition and such contestable witness as would never be admitted in a court of law are to be excluded those gaps will remain forever. I am a believer rather than a doubter, and I think there should be good reason before we dismiss any evidence, however slight. I would rather say something, even if it turns out to be wrong, for at least it can be disputed and something positive may come of it.

There are marked pieces — that is pieces bearing the signatures of identifiable artists. How secure are these? We know too well that in Chinese ceramics the practice of adding marks of earlier prestigious reigns was common; is it common in lacquer? Yet even false marks are evidence of something.

There are other less obvious aids. We may try to compare lacquer with porcelain, textiles or metal-work, to see if we can establish parallels and get at probable dates that way. That is a dangerous course but is sometimes fruitful. Or we can turn to literary sources, to written records, inventories and so on; they may prove that pieces of a certain type existed at a specified date but they do not prove that a piece recorded as being, for example, in a Japanese monastery in the thirteenth century is the one that is there now. Yet, all things being equal, it is reasonable to accept rather than to deny and to work on the assumption that a piece that was said to be in a certain treasure-house is likely to be the piece that is there still.

Political and social history may also give us clues. It is hardly likely, for instance, that when the Manchu were fighting with a brigand chief over the body of Beijing in 1640, lacquer-workers there would be producing their best work, or indeed any work at all. Subject-matter may equally limit possibilities. A landscape that includes a building known to have been constructed under the Ming cannot securely be given a Yuan date. The probable course of artistic and technical development has also to be considered; yet that too is less than certain, for sometimes skills improve from a primitive base and sometimes they deteriorate from a high one and what seems to be inevitable progression can equally be seen as inevitable retrogression.

All these clues can point where truth lies, but often they are contradictory and we are thrown back on subjective judgements. And that perhaps is no bad thing. The fascination of the study and pursuit of carved lacquer is largely the challenge that it offers to the mind as well as to the eye. No doubt when chemical and physical analysis of the material is more advanced it may become possible to say when and where a piece was made, but the chemist and the physicist will not be able to say whether it is beautiful or not.

CHAPTER 1

EARLY HISTORY: GURI WARE

In 1977 Chinese archaeologists working on a site of primitive culture in Zhejiang province discovered a wooden bowl coloured glossy red which tests showed to be more than 6,000 years old. The colorant was probably lacquer dyed with cinnabar, an ore of mercury mined in the provinces of Guizhou and Hunan.

Lacquer, a natural plastic, is the sap of the tree *Rhus verniciflua*, which exudes as a thick greyish-white liquid when the bark is cut. As lacquer ages it darkens to varying degrees of brown according to its quality, and when it solidifies, which it does in unusual conditions of fairly high humidity, it becomes extremely hard, takes a high polish, is resistant to damp and, very important in the Far East, repels the attentions of termites.

A material with such qualities was useful as a protective coating for wood, and when it was found that mixed with lamp-black, soot, Chinese ink, or meta-cinnabar (Burmeister, 1988) it could be given a brilliantly glossy surface, or mixed with cinnabar it became bright red, it was valued for its decorative quality. Both the sap in its natural state and cinnabar are poisonous, which, added to the belief in lacquer's efficacy as an elixir of life, was responsible for the esteem in which it was held.

Lacquer articles were at first a luxury dedicated to religious and royal use. According to literary tradition, the legendary Emperor Shun had his food and sacrificial vessels lacquered black whereas his successor caused his to be lacquered black on the outside but red within, an extravagance to which his advisers objected that 'a decorated lacquer dish costs ten times as much as a bronze one and yet is of no more use'.

China is a vast country and 6,000 years measured by Western standards is a long time. For much of that time we know little about how lacquer was used. The first solid information comes from archaeological work on Shang dynasty (*c.* 1600–1066 BC) sites. Material from tombs shows that lacquer was applied to wood as an adhesive into which were stuck pieces of turquoise or mother-of-pearl. In most cases the host vessel has rotted away or decayed, and the lacquer coat has survived only as a ghost impressed into the earth-shape of the body it covered. Some of the magnificent barbaric bronzes of the Shang and Zhou dynasties are known to have been coated with lacquer, their concavities picked out with a lacquer composition infill and the surface covered with another colour. Much later, in the Warring States period (480–221 BC), intricate three-dimensional wood-carvings were lacquered in a not dissimilar way.

Lacquer cannot be used in solid form because of its peculiar nature. Pure lacquer applied thinly will set extremely hard in the right conditions, but if used thickly the skin sets and the lacquer beneath remains malleable. One way of overcoming this difficulty was to adulterate the lacquer with ash and pig's blood or tong (paulownia) oil, so that a body was created that could be laid on thickly but because of the openness of its texture would set hard. Such a composition could be made deep enough to be modelled in relief or carved, but if the lacquer was heavily diluted it did not colour well, so a final coat of unadulterated lacquer was given. With rough wear this became thin and the brown-red body beneath was liable to show through; nevertheless, the adulterating of lacquer in some degree is an essential part of nearly all carved lacquer work.

The practice of lacquering, or trying to lacquer, relief objects seems to have been given up at about the time of the Former Han (206 BC–AD 8). Much lacquer made during that dynasty has been recovered from tombs. It is elaborately decorated in flat colours in a distinctive style that bears no relation to the carved lacquer of the Yuan (1279–1368) and the Ming (1368–1644) dynasties. Although most Han lacquer decoration is straightforwardly two-dimensional, a few examples show slightly raised ribbon-like shapes which were made by building up a thin layer of composition paste and then painting it with a contrasting colour. It is one of many instances of the Chinese yearning towards three-dimensional decoration.

One skin of lacquer is hard but many are harder. By the Warring States period (480–221 BC) lacquer was used to reinforce leather armour by laying one coat upon another. There is no proof that carvers made use of the extra depth of pure lacquer thus created until the Tang dynasty (618–907). In 1906 Sir Aurel Stein found among the ruins of Fort Miran in Turkestan some fragments of armour that had been carved. They consisted of small lacquer-coated leather plates that had been laced together after the manner of the jade burial suit of the Han princess (c. 100 BC) now in the Nanjing Museum. The lacquer had been applied in thirty-eight layers, each of which had been allowed to harden before the next was laid upon it. The depth achieved was not great but it was deep enough to be graved into a pattern of circular concavities, crescents, commas and S-shapes. It would be easy to suppose that some idle impressed soldier on tedious garrison duty had amused himself by carving his own or his commander's armour and thus gave rise to what later became a beautiful and sophisticated minor art; but it was not like that. It is clear that the carving was intended when the lacquer was applied for the skins are grouped together in seven bands of about five layers each: some groups are red-

brown, others black, so that when carved obliquely the recessed shapes in the bi-coloured mass are emphasised by the contrasting bands. If mere visibility was aimed at a top layer of black and the remainder of reddish-brown would have sufficed. Was there perhaps some regimental or hierarchic significance in the number of layers *(Pl. 1)*?

*Plate 1 **Fragments of Leather Armour***
Plaques, probably of camel-hide, lacquered in layers of red and black and carved through in 'comma' shapes, discovered by Aurel Stein in the ruins of Fort Miran. The armour was probably captured when the Tibetans overran Gansu in the eighth century. Tang. Length *c.* 10 cm.
British Museum

These unsophisticated carvings unearthed in a distant and dangerous outpost of the Chinese empire can hardly have been the beginning of carved lacquer. The technique of building up a thick body by applying layer after layer had been known for several centuries and though it was arduous and time-consuming it is unlikely to have been used only for proofing armour. No carved lacquer that is certainly earlier than the Fort Miran armour has come to light but it would be absurd to suppose that during the four centuries from the end of the Han to the beginning of the Tang the craft of lacquering did not develop. In the Lee Family collection is a covered box (Lee King Tsi, 1990: Pl. 1) which is said to be fifth-century AD. It is carved with curved designs through brownish-black, yellow, black and red lacquer to a brownish-black ground; and the rims are mounted with metal bands. Its general appearance suggests a Han piece but it is supposed that the carved shapes are of a post-Buddhist type and the box is therefore attributed to a period when Buddhism was popular in China. Although this is scarcely secure ground for the dating it is not difficult to accept that the box is very early.

*Plate 2 a, b **Mirror Box***
Black and red over a yellow ground. There is a false Wanli mark. The size and shape suggest it was designed to contain a metal mirror. No known fourteenth-century boxes have this combination of a scroll side and a diaper lid. Low Beer proposed Wanli but twelfth-/thirteenth-century? Diameter 17.5 cm, height 4.5 cm.
Linden-Museum, Stuttgart

Plate 3 ***Bowl-stand***
Red, black, yellow and green layers. Garner called it fifteenth-century (1979); Lee Yu-kuan called it twelfth-century (1972); a very similar bowl in the Los Angeles County Museum is called thirteenth-century (Kuwayama, 1982). The lightness, the wide shallow carving and the warping point to an early date. Twelfth-/thirteenth-century. Diameter 16 cm, height 6.5 cm.
British Museum

More interesting are two pieces from the Low Beer collection (Low Beer 1952: Pl. 52) now in the Linden-Museum in Stuttgart. One is a flat-topped box which seems to echo the central feature of Tang metal mirrors and is surely a mirror-box *(Pl. 2)*. It is quite distinct from the series of known Song guri lacquers.

It is not until the Song dynasty (960–1279) that we can date reasonably securely other pieces of carved lacquer. The most characteristic Song lacquer wares were functional pieces that depended on the harmonious relationship of simple shapes and smooth highly polished black or, less commonly, deep-brown surfaces. Such pieces often had as their sole concession to decoration a slightly raised line. So exquisite and puritan a taste, rooted in the Tang, could hardly have endured throughout two and a half centuries without change, so that towards the end of the Southern Song, the twelfth and thirteenth centuries, there were deviations towards more complex forms.

A number of Song texts mention carved lacquer but it is not certain what type of carved lacquer they refer to. It is generally believed to be the sort known by the Japanese as guri. The characteristic of guri lacquer is the recessing of abstract curving shapes variously and confusingly known as 'cloud pattern', 'brocade cloud', 'sword guard', 'ruyi-head' and so on, but which are essentially forms of repeating and confronting curves. Curvilinear patterning like this can be traced back

through many centuries, although not in lacquer. In its simplest form it is found in Tang silver-work and, somewhat grotesquely, carved into stoneware. Confusion over the term guri has been caused by the attempt to substitute in its place 'carved marbled lacquer', in reference to the stripes revealed by carving through contrasting colours. This does not help because representational lacquers also use contrasting colours in distinct layers and some guri lacquers are monochrome. The classic scrolls, or 'twisted grass', on the under-edge or cavetto of Yuan landscape and floral designs are commonly of one colour and reasonable people call them guri.

Among well-attested Song examples is a carved-lacquer mirror-case recovered from a Southern Song tomb in Jiangsu province that is thought not to be later than 1249 (Chen, 1979). It is not a beautiful object because the shape is ungainly, but the scroll-work has been reasonably well adjusted to the available space. The surface of this box is black, below it are, in order, three thick

layers of red, yellow and black, leading to a base of dark brown. It is carved obliquely and the bottom is rounded.

There is considerable variety in guri work but it remains on the whole unexciting and it is strange that a taste for it should have persisted so long. Many pieces seen today are eighteenth-century and some are modern. Not only may patterns vary; so may the range and order of colours, the size of each colour layer, the depth of lacquer and the style of carving, acute or oblique, with a V- or a U-shape at the bottom, and all may be clues to date.

Dating of guri is particularly difficult. According to the *Ge Gu Yao Lun* (published under the Ming in 1388 but perhaps written under the Yuan some twenty years earlier): 'Among ancient carved wares the most valuable have a burnished purple ground and show a reddish-black colour. The bottom is like an inverted roof-tile, they are lustrous, solid and thin. Less valued are those of which the colour is like that of a jujube, they are less valuable still when the carving is deep. Pieces which used to be made at Fuchou (Fuzhou) have a burnished yellow ground and circular patterns.' It is clear from this that by the mid-fourteenth century there was advanced connoisseurship in guri wares and that they were already spoken of as ancient.

*Plate 4 **Covered Box***
Guri pattern carved through layers of browns, reds and yellows. Clearly more sophisticated than plate 3, the carving is less shallow and the colour more evident. Dating of guri pieces is still largely subjective. This box has been related to a black and red rectangular panel (presumed pre-1321) recovered off the Sinan Coast of Korea, although the shape, a flattened sphere, seems more characteristic of Yongle/Xuande (*c.* 1420). Fourteenth- /fifteenth-century. Diameter 15.5 cm.
Bluett & Sons Ltd.

In the Nanjing Museum there is a shallowly carved dish, entirely black, which seems not to be carved lacquer but carved wood with a lacquer skin. Graving in wood preceded carving in lacquer and monochrome will certainly have been used before the sandwiching of colours; this dish could therefore be earlier than the Fort Miran fragments and the earliest piece of guri known.

Apart from the Lee family box already referred to, some of the apparently early lacquers that have survived without provenance may turn out to be earlier than has been claimed. Lee Yu-kuan (1972) illustrated a black bowl-stand that he held to be tenth-century. It was built up on alternate layers of red and black and had a 'flat' bottom. The base had a layer of white linen and the inside was lined with silvered copper. The carving he described as deep and rough. A similar bowl-stand in the British Museum is called 'fourteenth/fifteenth-century' *(Pl. 3)*.

*Plate 5 **Vase-stand***

From the damaged corners it can be seen that the original surface was black. A very narrow red guideline shows just clear of the composition that covers the wooden framework *(Pl. 6)*. The shallowness of the carving and the single colour argues for a very early date. The hole in the top to receive a vase was filled in later with a circle of brown-red lacquer diapered with concentric squares containing swastikas, to which has been applied a polychrome moulded decoration of fruit and leaves. At the same date the stand was covered with a skin of matching dull brown-red lacquer. Both colour and decoration are closely related to the vase with a Chongzhen mark

(Pl. 88). The reverse is in the original brown-black lacquer except for the circular inset which is black, thus confirming it to be a later addition, but whether of the mid-seventeenth century or the early twentieth is not clear. Lee Yu-kuan (1972) illustrates a similar stand of different dimensions with a centre constructed integrally which he describes as 'Japanese, Edo period, nineteenth-century, copied from an early Chinese form'. Twelfth- /thirteenth-century with, possibly, seventeenth-century additions. Length 16 cm, depth 7 cm. *Private collection*

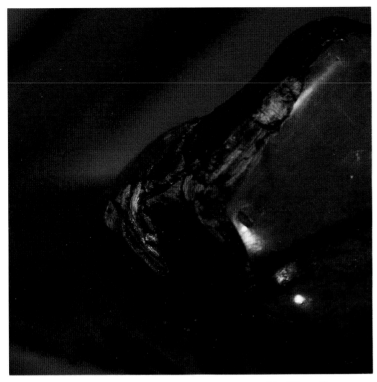

Plate 6 **Detail of Damaged Corner of Vase-stand in Plate 5**
The base is wood with a moderate thickness of grey composition on which are laid several coats of black, followed by a line of red and a final thicker band of black into which the pattern has been carved. A thin black line in early cinnabar pieces warns the carver that he is about to cut into the underlayer of composition, gesso, or bastard lacquer. Examples of black lacquer with a red guideline are less common.

If lightness, shallow carving and simple colour are signs of an early date then the vase-stand in plate 5 is certainly early, although it was altered in the late Ming by relacquering in dull brown-red and the insertion of a disk in the hole. A similar piece is illustrated by Lee Yu-kuan as Japanese of the nineteenth century but in that example the disk is integral with the stand and the surface is glossy black. There is no attempt in the stand to exploit different layers of colour. In its original form only the black would have been visible, an exceedingly narrow thread of red lacquer which runs through the black about nine-tenths of the way down was used solely as a guideline for the carver because it is placed at the very bottom of the cut and would have been almost if not entirely invisible *(Pl. 6)*. It has been suggested that the so-called 'guideline', which will be discussed later, developed out of the practice of sandwiching colours, as in the Fort Miran armour, but it is possible that the reverse is true. It may be that the shallow, broad U-shaped cut is characteristic of the mid-fourteenth century, the time when the guideline, commonly black in red, is first noticed in landscape dishes.

If we accept the evidence of the *Ge Gu Yao Lun* it would seem that the carving of the most valued guri was broad and shallow. Later — but still very early — wares were deep and heavy, and less well regarded. These perhaps were more accurately carved, resulting in a V-shaped cut. Later still, in the fourteenth century, the typical carving of guri seems to have become broad and shallow once again. Possibly both types were made throughout the period but in different centres.

Although occasional examples of guri carving appear on pieces that are certainly of the sixteenth or seventeenth century, the style does not seem to have been popular during the Ming dynasty when it was elbowed out by representational subjects. It was sometimes used again in the late eighteenth and nineteenth centuries, particularly in Japan, but the crisp lifelessness of the carving and the immaculate condition often betray its date and country of origin.

CHAPTER 2

MATERIALS AND WORKSHOP ORGANISATION

The author of the *Ge Gu Yao Lun* wrote of a certain make of guri as being 'deep but not strong', and elsewhere of the tendency of some other lacquers to crack and flake off. The quality of the lacquer and its condition when applied affect its stability, but it is also likely that substantial cracking and flaking is due to the foundation on which it is laid.

The body of the earliest lacquer wares may be wood, leather, bamboo, bronze, and perhaps stoneware. Wood was most commonly used, but wood insufficiently seasoned will contract and loosen the lacquer surface which cannot contract. Some woods are more stable than others. It is impossible without dismembering a piece of lacquer to determine what type of wood has been used. Species that have been mentioned are pine, paulownia, willow, elm and camphor (Lee, 1972). Even seasoned wood, if the lacquer has been damaged and the water-resistant skin broken, is liable to move. To reduce weight and to lessen the chances of movement, the wooden foundation was pared down as thinly as possible. If the wood was covered with a layer of lacquer composition — powdered ashes mixed with pig's blood or tong oil, which unlike pure lacquer dried evenly — a light, strong body was available for the lacquerer. The composition varied according to the ingredients used, the proportion of pig's blood and the nature of the

ashes which might be fine or coarse, of one sort or another. Powdered brick of three different grades of fineness was at one time used as a standard mix.

The foundation of the box-lid in plate 7 is light wood. The upper surface is covered with a thin coat of composition on which are laid successive layers of red lacquer deep enough for carving in relief. The underside of the lid is treated with a much thicker coating of composition which has been finished with polished black lacquer. The grey composition on this box probably contains wood ash; powdered brick is denser in texture and darker in colour with a hint of red.

Another method was to use fabric to give tensile strength to the lacquer skin and lessen the danger of cracking. Materials identified are linen, hemp and silk, but a fine fabric woven from ramie, a plant of the nettle family, was most common. The fabric was impregnated with lacquer and pasted on to the foundation. After it had set hard a layer of composition was applied which was then ground smooth in preparation for lacquering *(Pl. 8)*.

In the method known as 'dry lacquer' the wooden body was replaced with a temporary one of unbaked clay. As with the lost-wax process of bronze casting, the temporary body, the clay, was washed away after the lacquer

Plate 7 **Detail of Box-lid in Plate 57**
The damaged edge shows, in sequence: a vermilion upper skin, a brown-red layer, more vermilion, a line of dark brown-red, yet another layer of vermilion, a shallow composition ground, whitish fabric, wood, blue cloth, a thick layer of composition, the glossy black surface of the interior. Inferior or second-hand Chinese cloth was often dyed blue (Lee, 1972).

Plate 8 **Detail of Small Saucer**
This shows the use of material to give tensile strength to a composition body. On either side of the coarse cloth is a layer of dark grey composition covered with a layer of dark red lacquer. Early Qing. Diameter 12 cm.
Private collection

had set and the skin — hard, strong and light — was left as a record of the underlying shape.

Far less often than upon wood, lacquer was laid upon a ceramic body. There is an example in the National Palace Museum of an Yixing stoneware teapot that has been submerged in carved red lacquer, not to its advantage. There is another in the Palace Museum at Beijing and I have seen similar modern plastic-covered pieces in Hollywood Road, Hong Kong. A well-known example is illustrated in plate 89.

In the *Ge Gu Yao Lun* is a sentence that has been translated as: 'Many lacquer pieces of the Song imperial court were done in unadorned gold or silver.' This has been taken to mean that gold and silver vessels were totally covered in lacquer, to which it has been objected that it was absurd to cover up precious metals. But, in fact, it would be perfectly reasonable to protect with lacquer the outside of gold and silver drinking cups, which were thin and delicate, leaving the metal exposed inside. The libation cup in plate 9 shows how gilded metal liners were still used in the late fifteenth century although by that time the coating of a metal body with lacquer had been replaced by the lining of a lacquer body with metal. Modern lacquer made commercially in Beijing is usually on a brass foundation that has been enamelled bright blue on the inside *(Pl. 122)*.

Type of foundation is not a reliable guide to date as there is no reason why an early method or its variant could not be used at any later time and in any lacquer-making centre. The dry-lacquer process was not much used after the seventeenth century except for some modern figures made at Fujian. Very heavy pieces that suggest the presence of a body such as lead are often, but not always, of the eighteenth or nineteenth century. It has been said that a heavy body was sometimes used to trick collectors into thinking that was gold (Lee, 1972). I doubt this. Lead was used as a base for lacquer as early as the tenth century and the box in plate 116 was certainly not made with an intention to deceive.

A Chinese connoisseur of the twelfth century, Cheng Dachang, wrote that lacquerers in his time used only three colours whereas in the fourth century five were used. His evidence of the practice in his own day may be accepted but the five colours of the earlier period were probably oil-bound paint rather than lacquer. It has also been said that in Song and Yuan times lacquer colours were limited to red, black and yellow, and that green was not added until the later Ming when a different shade of red was introduced. This is broadly true but it may be that some pieces in which green is used are earlier than is at present supposed.

Reds vary from bright vermilion to dull reddish-brown, almost to a chestnut or mahogany colour. Colour may be a clue to dating but, like other clues, it cannot by itself be proof. The glowing deep red typical of Yuan and early Ming lacquer was attempted at later periods; and the dull brown-reds of the later Ming were also used again in the mid-Qing. These brown-reds do not occur on fourteenth- and fifteenth-century wares, unless they have been relacquered as in the vase-stand in plate 6. Nor do the bright vermilions of the Qing appear before, at the earliest, the mid-seventeenth century.

Lacquer may vary in quality according to where it is grown, the time of year at which it is harvested, how it is stored and whether it has been taken in the accepted way by making incisions in the bark of the tree or by boiling its twigs. If it is used without additive, as it is on the base of many early pieces, the colour of the purest lacquer is dark tortoiseshell, has a rich shiny surface, is slightly translucent and does not crack. The quality of the lacquer sap and the amount of colorant used resulted in variations. The Chinese are great experimenters and we do not certainly know what other means they may have taken to modify too fresh a red; it has been said that cassia juice, an oil of cinnamon, was

Plate 9 **Libation Cup**
The yellow ground does not curl away from the base as in earlier pieces. The fruit and foliage design, although adjusted to the space available, springs from outside its frame. It has a low ridged foot rim and a black lacquered base with a slightly depressed centre. The interior is lined with silver metal that has been gilded. A not dissimilar cup — with feet — in the collection of Low Beer was called by him 'probably sixteenth-century'. In the City of Aberdeen Museum there is a red lacquer guri cup lined with metal (silver, pewter or tin) with a similarly depressed base that has the appearance of considerable age and for which, were it not for the likeness to this cup, a much earlier date might have been suggested. Other footed libation cups are in Boston and the Victoria and Albert Museum. Possibly Chenghua. Length including handle 11.5 cm, width 6.1 cm, depth 3.8 cm.
Private collection

sometimes added on its own to give a different, darker colour.

Another source of variation may be the adding of tong oil, which speeded setting and deepened red but not black. Bright glossy black is not a natural colour of lacquer but is achieved with additives. Many pieces, chiefly late eighteenth- or nineteenth-century but also some early examples, have a dull black base spotted with impurities. These bases have probably been treated with a low-grade lacquer made from boiling twigs. Black sets less quickly than red and individual coats, if they lack tong oil, are probably thinner. Black is also a better reflector of light than red and when not adulterated takes a higher gloss. The most brilliant of Song monochromes are black. Bases of pieces that have been in Japanese collections have often been relacquered. They can be recognised by their shiny uncracked surface, although not all this relacquering of bases is Japanese. Some cracking is usually found on the bases of pieces of the seventeenth century and earlier if they have not been relacquered.

Colour may be fugitive. The effect of sunlight on red lacquer has not generally been remarked. It is said that a twelfth-century monochrome box when recovered from a tomb was a lustrous coral red that later darkened; and a nineteenth-century box darkened merely from being exposed for a few months on an occasionally sunlit window-sill whereas the undercurve of the box, being in shade, remained in a higher key. The Japanese keep their highly valued lacquer in padded boxes to protect them not only from casual damage but also from the harmful effects of sunlight.

Such cautionary tales should not be allowed to mislead. Clearly, no rare, beautiful and valuable object should be dropped or banged about, but lacquer is exceedingly tough, presumably when used on armour it was banged about a good deal. It does chip if roughly used, but the practice of entombing all lacquer objects in padded boxes is unnecessary. It is an instance of what Roger Fry called the Chinese device of getting the observer into a suitable frame of mind for an aesthetic experience. If the preparation is sufficiently arcane the aesthetic experience is assured. Care when carried to great lengths is merely ludicrous.

One museum that has a considerable collection puts none of it on view and is reluctant to allow anyone to see it. The practice of equipping oneself with kid gloves when handling lacquer is absurd. What is supposed to have been the life of a lacquer bowl, dish, tray, box or table when it was made? Valued it certainly was, but not to the point of folly.

Plate 10 **Detail of Wood-based Box in Plate 108**
Shows the foundation of wood upon which is laid a skin of lacquer-impregnated material followed by grey composition. The wood in the lid is several times thicker than in the body of the box.

Carved lacquer objects that have been about the world for several hundred years need to be cared for, not cosseted. Painted or gilded lacquer is another matter. The harmful effects of sunlight may depend upon the quality of lacquer. Some lacquers discolour quickly, others not. It is wise to keep all lacquer out of direct sunlight but normal daylight or artificial lighting rarely does any harm. Nor is there any need to be over-zealous in creating a constant temperature for storage. If lacquer had been so delicate as to require closely controlled air conditions very little would have survived. The climate in China has as great extremes as any likely to be encountered.

Before we explore further it should be said that a given piece of lacquer was usually not the creation of one person, the artist, rather it was a factory product that involved several different crafts. There is an inscribed winged cup of the Han dynasty in the British Museum that reads:

Fourth year of Yuanshi (AD 4). Shu Commandery, West Factory. Imperial cup of wood, lacquered, engraved and painted, with gilded handles. Capacity one *sheng*, sixteen *yue*. Initial work, Yi; application of lacquer, Li; top work, Deng; gilding of bronze handles, Gu; painting, Ding; engraving, Feng; finishing, Ping; production, Zong Zao. Official in charge of the soldiers of the factory guard, Zhang; Manager, Liang; Deputy, Feng; Assistant, Long; Head clerk, Bao Zhu.

Apart from the construction of the wooden or clay body, fine and critical work that in the case of the Han cup was carried out by the artificer Yi, and the patient skill of Li who laid layer upon layer of lacquer and polished each one before applying the next, two additional members of the team were necessary: the designer and the carver. It certainly may have happened (and later probably did in certain ateliers) that both functions were carried out by the same person, but it was rare. The carvers of lacquers of late fourteenth- and early fifteenth-century lacquers worked from designs doled out to the production line on the shop floor just as they are today. Anyone who has seen the modern Chinese workshop will recognise the system. The design to be copied — whether in silk, bronze or sandalwood — lies on the table before the craftsman and from that he works, deviating only because even the most painstaking cannot avoid it. The designer was not the carver; he was essentially a worker in two dimensions and although he might create his design with relief in mind, it was on a flat surface he created it as he would when painting a picture or designing a fabric. It was up to the carver to adjust the design drawn by an artist who might not have fully understood the technical limitations of the medium. Once the carver's work was completed, the polisher took over.

It is probable that the patterns of the earliest carved lacquers derived from those drawn for other purposes. Only later, when the art was well-established, will it have developed its own corps of specialist designers.

CHAPTER 3

SONG AND YUAN CARVED LACQUER

The patterns on the earliest carved lacquers were abstract; figurative and floral pieces came later, and yet perhaps not so much later as has been thought. It is reported that a dish of carved red lacquer on a gilded silver and lead base was recovered from the tomb of Wang Jian, who died in 918 during the Five Dynasties period (907–960), but as the lacquer had largely come away from the body and there is no account of what the carving represented, the value of the discovery is limited (Feng, 1961). The carving may have been of the guri type but the report fails to make this clear. A small carved lacquer box decorated with flying dragons on a gold ground bearing the mark of Zhenghe of the Northern Song (1111–17) is said to be in a private collection (Shi, 1957). If these two pieces are carved and really exist they would go a long way to establishing the beginning of representational carved lacquer far earlier than has been supposed. Instead, we must build our ideas around pieces about which more is known.

The earliest is a dish in the Sackler Gallery of the Smithsonian Institute, Washington *(Pl. 11)*. The lacquer is in bands of black and dark red, shallowly carved with four phoenixes surrounding a peony flower. There is a paired key-fret on the inner rim and a band of flowers on the underside. The material appears to be lacquer mixed with composition, for Lee Yu-kuan described it as 'coarse with fine grains glittering in it like golden stars'. The brown base, which has an 'orange-peel' appearance, bears characters that may be differently interpreted but are thought to imply a date of 1216 or 1289 (Lee, 1972).

We are on rather more firm ground with two pieces that the records of the Engakuji Temple in Japan claim to have been brought there in 1279 by a famous travelling monk, Xu Ziyuan, who arrived in Kamakura in that year (Okada, 1969). The first is a large landscape dish, known as 'The Pavilion of a Drunken Old Man' *(Pl. 12)*.

Another piece, 'Boys Playing in a Moonlit Garden', stylistically related to plate 12, is in the Tokyo National Museum. It is even lighter and shallower than the other two pieces and may have been made earlier, perhaps towards the end of the Southern Song at Hangzhou or Wenzhou where there are known to have been workshops at the time *(Pl. 13)*.

These three pieces in many respects hang together but a fourth, which has a good claim to belong to the same date, is rather different. In the Engakuji is a domed incense box with the same reputed provenance as plate 13 (Okada, 1969). It is decorated with two peafowl flying among peonies. It is in two shades of red, a deep

Plate 11 **The Four Phoenixes Dish**

Layers of alternating black and dark red. The red is adulterated and is said to have 'fine grains glittering in it like golden stars' (Lee, 1972). An inscription on the reverse, not contemporary, appears to date the dish to 1216. It bears the reign mark of an emperor whose reign title was Antang but there is a discrepancy between the reputed date of his death and the date on this dish. Antang came from Dalifu in the Dali kingdom of Yunnan and if

this dish, which is undoubtedly very early, is of Antang's reign it is not improbable that this and related pieces are representatives of lacquer ware known as 'Old Yunnan'. It is shallowly carved in bastard lacquer, a material in which coloured lacquer is heavily adulterated with ash. The key-fret border is coupled, not continuous. Song. Diameter 35.4 cm, depth 3.8 cm.

Arthur M. Sackler Collection, Smithsonian Institute, Washington DC

Plate 12 **Dish: The Pavilion of a Drunken Old Man**
Black lacquer against a buff ground, carved with a landscape
framed with a narrow black rouleau; beyond is a broad border of
flowers and foliage inconsequentially arranged in an open way. The
dish is edged with a broader black rouleau. Traditionally said to
have been brought to the Engakuji Temple in 1279 by the travelling monk Xu Ziyuan, who arrived in Kamakura in that year. An inventory of 1363 seems to refer to this among other pieces. It is light
and thin like the dish in plate 13. Southern Song. Diameter 36 cm.
Engakuji Temple, Kamakura

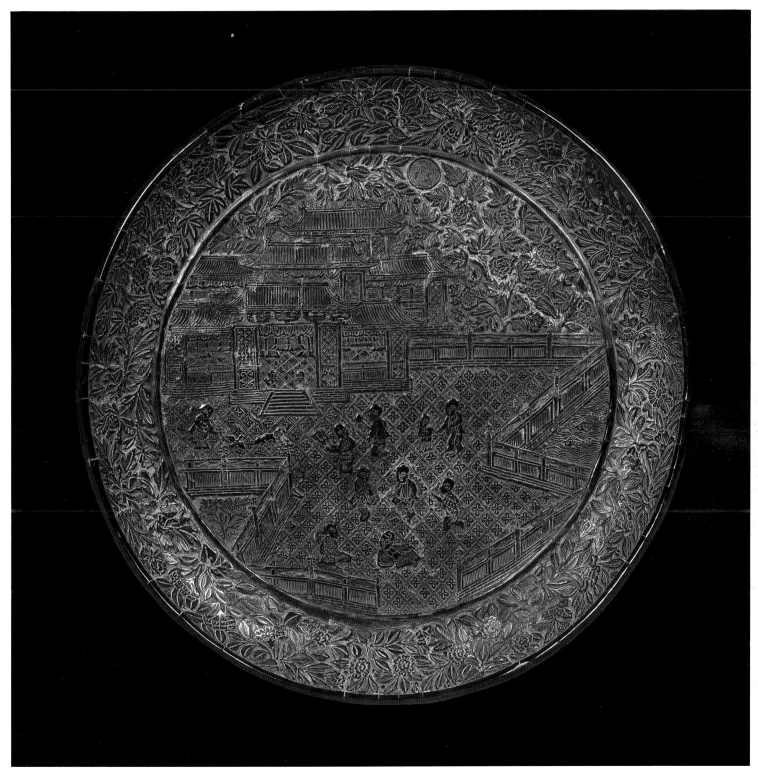

Plate 13 **Dish: Boys Playing in a Moonlit Garden**

Lee Yu-kuan, who handled the piece, describes it as on a lacquer-soaked cloth foundation (1972). The top layer is of brownish-black natural coloured lacquer with an 'amber-like lustre', followed by a thin bright red line and a thick layer of natural lacquer mixed with ash, all on an undecorated buff ground. It is not clear if the buff ground was laid directly upon the cloth foundation; probably not. The landscape is framed with a narrow rouleau, beyond is a border of leaves and flowers openly arranged. Although the ground is symbolised by square diapers enclosing a four-petalled flower, and water by the humped wave form, the air space is filled with flowers and leaves shown naturalistically sprouting from behind a garden fence and reaching out of the picture space and back again into it. A corner of land outside the garden is occupied in the same way. A closely related tray, but red on yellow, illustrating 'The Red Cliff' poem was shown in the *Art of the Muromachi Period Exhibition*, Tokyo National Museum, 1989. The dish is edged with a rouleau of natural lacquer. Song. Diameter 31.2 cm, depth 4.5 cm.

Tokyo National Museum

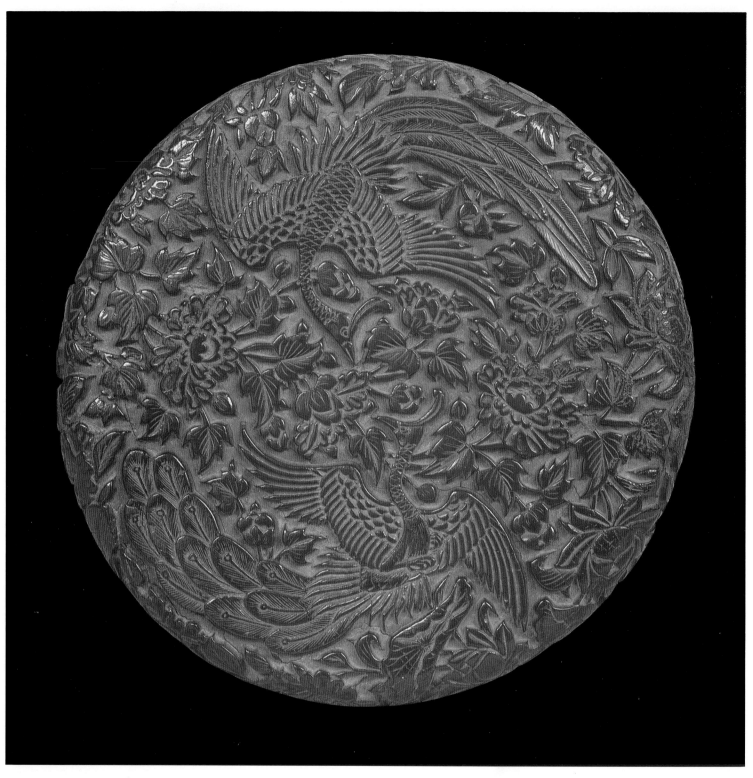

Plate 14 **Domed Incense Box**
Two peafowl flying among loosely arranged foliage and flowers, probably peonies. The rich rose-red lacquer is in two tones, the undecorated ground is several tones lighter than the surface. The carving appears to be deeper than in the other pieces of this group and the edges are fully rounded. The Engakuji inventory of 1363 records a dish like this traditionally brought to the monastery by the travelling monk Xu Ziyuan when he arrived in Kamakura in 1279. Song. Diameter 17.5 cm.
Engakuji Temple, Kamakura

Plate 15 **Bowl and Stand**

A thin skin of brown-black lacquer over a yellow-red composition. The oblique carving has the effect of emphasising the features of the design. The key-fret border, used twice on the bowl and once on the stand, is of an early type found on Yuan porcelain in which no fret connects with its neighbour. The stand has a simple interlocking fret like that on the lid of a guri box in the same museum which is also a Song piece. The base of the stand is decorated with parallel vertical lines that suggest basket-work or formalised petals. The bowl is lined with metal, silver or pewter, and the bottom of the foot rim is reinforced with the same metal. The top of the stand is divided into four matching cartouches of flowers and leaves separated by a ground of unusual diapers. Song. Bowl: height 10.1 cm, diameter 20.8 cm. Stand: length 9.2 cm, diameter 19.3 cm. *Linden-Museum, Stuttgart*

rose-red against a lighter undecorated ground. Unlike the other pieces it has no black outer skin. The rounded carving and the box shape suggest an advance in skill and sophistication. If this was made before 1279 the others should be earlier still *(Pl. 14).*

Several other pieces can reasonably be associated with this group. The most remarkable is the bowl and stand at one time in the Low Beer collection, where it was thought to be seventeenth-century (Low Beer, 1952), and now in the Linden-Museum, Stuttgart (Brandt, 1988). Once more there is a brown-black skin laid over a great depth of adulterated lacquer coloured Indian red. The oblique carving into the mass gives a brown-red appearance to the whole and has the effect of separating the units of the design so that they look distinct *(Pl. 15).*

Four of this group — the two landscape dishes, the dish with the four phoenixes, and the bowl and stand — have a certain likeness of colour: a black surface skin carved through to a yellowish red. The provenance of the fifth, the rose-red incense box, links it to the others. A significant feature common to all is the use of a heavily adulterated lacquer for the main layer.

The landscape dishes have obvious common features. Each is encircled by a broad band of leaves and flowers separated from the centre by a narrow raised line. The species of plant is not identical but the components are small and set against a plain ground without overlapping, each leaf and flower is drawn in plan and does not fold over upon itself as it would in nature. In 'Boys Playing in a Moonlit Garden' this rather primitive treatment spills over into the landscape itself, an engagingly childlike device that is not repeated in 'The Pavilion of a Drunken Old Man'. Both landscapes are crowded and 'busy'. They need to be read rather than seen. They are probably the product of the same workshop at very nearly the same date.

'The Four Phoenixes' dish *(Pl. 11)* differs in that there is no floral band but instead a much narrower key-fret edging. The long-tailed birds disport themselves symmetrically around a large peony flower and the remainder of the background is scattered indiscriminately with disconnected foliage. Once again there is the impression that the designer felt the need to fill all his available space. It is this crowded design, together with the colour, the lightness and the shallowness of the carving, that marks it as being not far removed in time from the landscape dishes. The key-fret, which does not appear on the other dishes, is in the coupled or early form. The key-fret on the bowl and stand is not coupled but of a type earlier still, in which the frets are discrete.

To these pieces, which circumstances suggest we must call Song, there can be added three others. One in the Tokugawa Art Museum has an inscription dating it to 1268; another in the Tokyo National Museum is inscribed with the maker's name but no date (Okada, 1989); and a third, inscribed with the same maker's name as the second and the date 1294 (or conceivably 1234), is in Boston (Boston Museum of Fine Arts, 1982). These can easily be related to each other and to the Engakuji examples.

The range of decoration in these pieces suggests that the output of these thirteenth-century workshops may have been large, although few have survived.

CHAPTER 4

THE SINAN POTICHE AND FLORAL PATTERNS

There are two further pieces that we can securely date to before the middle of the fourteenth century. The first of these is the 'Sinan Potiche'.

The Sinan Potiche *(Pl. 16)* was recovered from a wreck off the Sinan Coast of Korea in 1967. From other material in the wreck it has been dated to no later than 1321. It had lain under seventy feet of sea-water for 650 years and had come to little harm. With it on the sea-bed were a panel and a fan handle, both of guri design in black and red (National Museum of Korea, 1977).

There is a gap of only about half a century between the peacock and peony box in the Engakuji and this small pot, but the leap in style and technique is great. With its close covering of a difficult surface that is curved in two directions and its naturalistic treatment of the peony, the petals folded back on themselves, it could hardly have sprung fully armed from the soil. The contrast between this and the Engakuji pieces suggests a different ancestry. Not only is the potiche carved on layered rather than bastard lacquer, but the style is so dissimilar that the later cannot be seen as a development of the earlier. What were its predecessors and why is it so different from the other group?

In the first quarter of the fourteenth century, a time of vigorous development in the arts and in foreign trade,

the famous blue-and-white porcelain was first made. It is natural to ask if there was cross-fertilisation of one art by another, but blue-and-white was essentially a painted art dealing in surfaces whereas lacquer, which had been flat-painted under the Han, was seeking to explore the possibilities of relief. It is therefore not to blue-and-white that we should look for the immediate ancestors of the Sinan Potiche, but to the three-dimensional moulded and engraved porcelain Ding bowls of the twelfth and thirteenth centuries and further back still to the patterns of embroidered silks.

Moulds made as negatives to be impressed on the inner face of Ding wares still survive. There are two examples in the British Museum, one in the Percival David Collection and another in the Asian Art Museum of San Francisco. They have patterns of flowers — lotus, peony or chrysanthemum; in the Percival David mould, which is dated 1184 *(Pl. 17)*, there are phoenixes, and in the British Museum example of 1203 (Riddell, 1979) there is a classic scroll border. The San Francisco example is dated 1301 *(ibid.)*. Lacquer cannot be cast in a mould as porcelain can (no doubt, the Chinese being adventurous experimentalists, it was attempted), yet the idea of creating similar reliefs in so valued a material was in the air of the thirteenth century. These ceramic moulds are the immediate predecessors of the Sinan Potiche.

Where was it made? The capital of the Southern Song was Hangzhou and the industrial powerhouse of the empire was the Yangtze valley. The Yuan who supplanted them established their capital at modern Beijing but the manufacture and trading centre remained in the basin of the great river that flows into the eastern sea. Because of the relationship between the folded petals of the peony on the potiche and those on the reliefs of, say, contemporary celadons it would be reasonable to suppose that the potiche was made in the general neighbourhood of the famous porcelain kilns in the Yangtze basin where river transport and ports for overseas trade were available.

The potiche was presumably a sample that never reached its destination and generated no orders, but there are other pieces of early carved lacquer of essentially ceramic shape. A fine leys jar in the Palace Museum, Beijing *(Pl. 18)*, presented even greater difficulties for the carver and is a well-known ceramic form, and three rather similar long-necked bottles — one in the BASF Collection in Munster *(Pl. 19)*, another very like it in the National Palace Museum, Taiwan (National Palace Museum, 1971), and a third in the British Museum *(Pl. 20)* — are based on potters' shapes. Curiously, no bowl shapes in representational lacquer attributable to an early date have yet been identified. Although these vase and bottle shapes are not as early as the potiche they have some claims to be called Yuan, and there are several dishes and boxes with flower, or flower-and-bird, designs that are stylistically related to the potiche and may pre-date it.

*Plate 16 a, b **The Sinan Lidded Potiche***
Recovered from the Sinan Coast of Korea in 1976 from a wreck that lay under seventy feet of water, the earliest flower-patterned carved lacquer so far identified. Not later than 1321. Height 7 cm. *National Museum of Korea, Seoul*

There is no obvious connection between the potiche and the guri lacquers that were found with it; they are both carved lacquer and that is the end of it. Later we shall find arabesque carvings in the form of classic scrolls under the cavetto of floral dishes and in association with landscapes.

There was a stage when lacquer workers in one mode learned to work in others. The remarkable dish (Krahl and Morgan, 1989) in plate 21 shows a marriage between *qiangjin* lacquer (a technique of engraving a design upon lacquer and filling it with gold that is well proven to have been practised during the Southern Song) and a carved border of flowers and leaves lying in a rather open manner in plan against a plain ground, with, on the underside of the cavetto, an early form of classic scroll. Equally interesting is the box in Stuttgart (Brandt, 1988: Pl. 20) where the sides are carved with a repeating lotus feature and the top with a pair of phoenixes against an involved lotus background. On the sloping border to the lid is carved a running key-fret at an angle, a most unusual feature. This should be Northern Song or Tang. Another dish which seems to be related (Tokyo National Museum, 1977: Pl. 442) has a pair of phoenixes against an open background of trailing leaves and flowers of uncertain species. Once again the border is idiosyncratic.

Plate 17 **Stoneware Mould**
An unglazed mould for impressing decoration on the inside of
bowls. On the concave side it is dated 1184. Diameter 21.9 cm.
Percival David Foundation

Plate 18 **Leys Jar**

Signed by Yang Mao, who flourished in the late Yuan and early Ming. Yang Mao is thought to have been a member of a family that specialised in lacquer-making in Yanghui village, Xietang, Jiaxing prefecture, Zhejiang province. His work is said to have been eagerly acquired in the Ryukyu Islands and in Japan, from where it is alleged that examples were returned to China as tribute in the middle of Yongle's reign. Although much faked, this signature is thought to be genuine. Yuan. Height, 9.4 cm, diameter 12.8 cm.
Palace Museum, Beijing

Plate 19 **Mallet-shaped Vase**

Flowers of the four seasons are carved in a close design against a yellow ground. There is a black guideline. The interior is brown lacquer; the base has been relacquered black. A similar vase (height 16.4 cm) in Taibei (National Palace Museum, 1972) has a plain rim dividing the body from the neck, and a band of coupled key-fret in place of the *lingzhi*, magic mushrooms, around the collar. The Taibei vase bears a scratched Yongle mark on the base but, because of its likeness to the Sinan Potiche *(Pl. 16)* and the coupled key-fret, I prefer a Yuan date. Yuan. Height 15.5 cm.
BASF Lacquer Museum, Munster

Plate 20 **Ring-necked Vase**

There is a Xuande mark over a partly erased Yongle one. Garner attributed this to the first half of fifteenth century (1979), but it may well be a century earlier. The decoration is of red flowers against a plain buff ground. There is a coupled key-fret around the foot rim and a petalled border which is repeated below the bamboo-ribbed chimney. Yuan. Height 10.7 cm.
British Museum

From this point we can show a number of dishes that have flower, or flower-and-bird, patterns on the main surface and more developed classic scrolls under the cavetto. The dating of these is not easy. One indication is the degree of sophistication in the drawing: flowers and leaves that are set out in plan at one level are earlier than those in which the leaves fold back upon themselves, or lie on different planes. Designs that are well-integrated and evolve naturally within the picture space show an increase of skill and confidence *(Pl. 23)*.

Black is more common than red and is generally earlier. Black was the favoured colour of the visually puritan Song but was not popular with the Ming, the 'bright' dynasty. There are no black flower dishes in the vast secret collection of the Qing court in the Palace Museum in Beijing (Palace Museum, 1985) although there are red ones. The Ming court moved north in 1421 and no doubt took with them lacquer from their store in Nanjing; we should expect the Beijing hoard to contain only Ming and Qing pieces and possibly a few late Yuan ones, so it is to be presumed that the absence of black dishes is because they were no longer made.

If these carved black lacquer dishes are Song why are they not found in their tombs? Simple, workaday black lacquers have been recovered in quantities; were these highly worked dishes too valuable to be entrusted to the dead? Or were they too frivolous? The reasonable conclusion is that they are not Song but Yuan.

Garner's attribution of densely designed dishes of this sort to the Yuan was widely accepted, but not by Low Beer whom Garner regarded as a great contributor to lacquer studies. Low Beer thought most of them were either of the seventeenth century or Japanese copies (Low Beer, 1977). The grounds of his disagreement were that the patterns lacked the coherence that was always to be looked for in Chinese art. Garner admitted some incoherence existed but argued unconvincingly that greater control of the pattern was the consequence of increasing Ming influence (Garner, 1979).

There is a difference in quality among these pieces and it may be that some are copies made in the seventeenth century, possibly in Japan. But, in the main, Garner's attribution of many of them to the fourteenth century is right.

In trying to establish a sequence for this group one must consider the quality of the lacquer, its colour and thickness, the skill of the carver and signs of age, but each, on its own, is an unreliable guide; to depend on any one of them allows nothing for the idiosyncrasies of individual artists, or for temporary problems such as interruptions of supply of materials.

Plate 21 a, b **Qiangjin** *Tray*

This may represent an early stage in the development of carved lacquer (Krahl and Morgan, 1989). It has been compared with a tray
in Boston (Museum of Fine Arts, 1982) that is dated 1234 or 1294,
but the similarities are not great although both are evidently early.
The *qiangjin* decoration on this piece implies sophisticated craftsmanship, but the guri carving is less developed. Southern Song.
Length 30.7, width 15.7 cm.
Bluett & Sons Ltd.

Plate 22 *Flower and Bird Dish*

Deep carving through black lacquer to a buff ground. The long-tailed birds have no detailed feathering on head and body, a feature found in some dishes otherwise similar. The line of their backs is uncomfortably out of harmony with the sweep of the tails and the general movement of the design. This dish is very similar to a black dish in Seattle (National Palace Museum, 1987: Pl. 59) and to a red one in Beijing (Palace Museum, 1985: Pl. 10), but its inferiority is apparent. Is the plainness of the birds characteristic of an individ-ual carver or workshop? Ostensibly Yuan. Diameter 32 cm. For diameter of such dishes exported to Japan see Figgess 1962–63. *Fitzwilliam Museum, Cambridge*

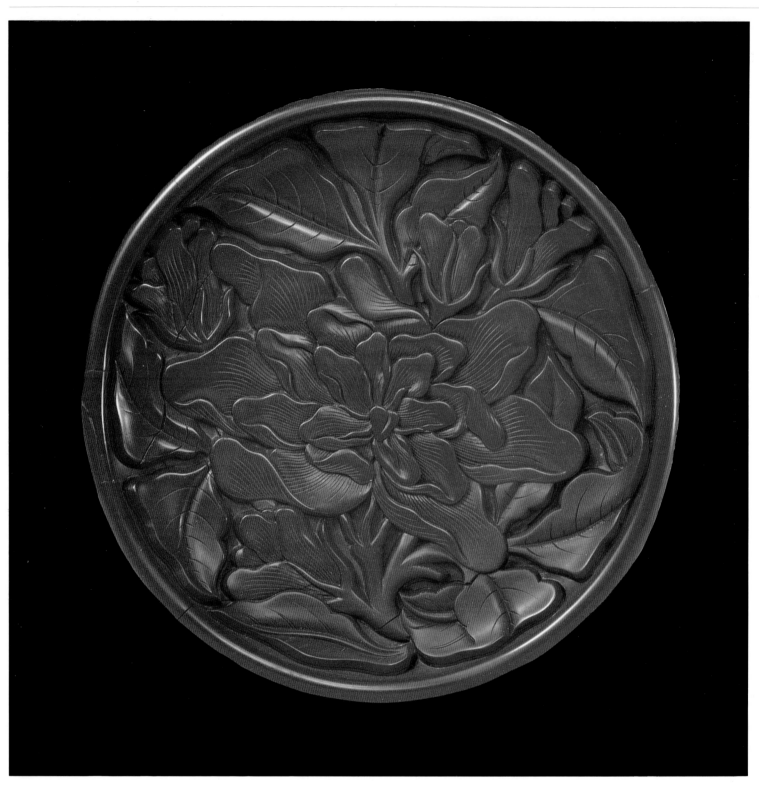

Plate 23 **Dish**

A bold design of gardenias in red against a plain buff ground. The reverse of the cavetto is carved with a classic scroll. The base is signed Zhang Cheng, one of the two artists named in the *Ge Gu Yao Lun*. Like Yang Mao *(Pl. 18)*, he is thought to have operated in the lacquer-making centre in Zhejiang. Yuan. Diameter 16.5 cm, depth 2.6 cm.
Palace Museum, Beijing

Plate 24 **Small Table**
This magnificent piece is the earliest of the three notable pieces of
lacquer furniture formerly in the collection of Low Beer. A very
similar stool or low table is in Beijing (Palace Museum, 1985: Pls.
48, 49). Hongwu? Length 53 cm, width 21 cm, height 14.8 cm.
Museum für Ostasiatische Kunst, Berlin

Plate 25 **Large Dish**
There is a six-character Xuande mark, but it may be earlier. This
piece is remarkable for its variety of flowers: peony, gardenia,
camellia, chrysanthemum, lotus, waterweed, peach and cherry blossom. The Xuande Emperor himself was a flower painter, which argues in favour of the date of the mark. Without the mark it might
have been thought to be earlier. Xuande. Diameter 54.3 cm, depth
6.2 cm.
Ashmolean Museum, Oxford

Plate 26 **Red Dish**
An ordered circular design that is not directional is uncommon. A
very similar dish in Beijing is there called Yongle. This dish is called
'late Ming (early 17th century)' for which there seems to be little
justification because it lacks the unsympathetic harshness of design
characteristic of most Jiajing lacquer. Mid-fifteenth-century, possibly Chenghua. Diameter 29.5 cm, depth 4.5 cm.
Avery Brundage Collection, Asian Art Museum of San Francisco

Those examples in the Palace Museum that the authorities in Beijing call Yuan (Pl. 23) show the folded leaf and a certain crowded naturalness and are distinguished from the pieces that we call Yongle and Xuande by being less 'arranged' as patterns (Pl. 25). A curious feature common to all but the earliest floral pieces of this type is the presence of at least one leaf, sometimes two or three, in which the central rib is in relief. This feature is repeated almost as though it were an atelier mark; in the Beijing dish it can be clearly seen on the lowest leaf, but in some later pieces the raised rib may be on either the back or the front of the leaf in that arbitrary way which is the mark of the copyist, the consequence of a misunderstanding of the original design.

Another detail that may be significant in helping to establish a date concerns the secondary veins of the leaves. On those with a concave main rib the ancillaries are carved so that they widen towards their base, but when the rib is raised the ancillaries are represented by two lines which leave the main rib and meet at a point. On pieces that may be of slightly later date, say 1430 as against 1390, the veins to the ribs that are proud of the leaf are represented by two converging knife strokes that do not always meet, and the veins to most others are of even thickness throughout, although on the earliest we know, the Sinan potiche, the leaf-veins are shown as a simple groove.

A circular plate or box-lid, whatever the material, should ideally have no north or south, whichever way it is presented it should look right; its circularity should be respected and we should not need to swivel it round to look at it. The designs on Yuan porcelain plates and on most early Ming bird-and-flower pieces do not obey this rule; they remain inescapably directional because of the main stem and shape of the flower. If we give the piece a half or quarter turn it is difficult to see the design with equal pleasure because we are at once aware that there is a right way up. When flower-heads are arranged symmetrically emphasising the decorative rather than the representational nature of the design, as in plate 26, the piece is probably from the second half of the fifteenth century.

CHAPTER 5

THE REN TOMB BOX AND THE SOCIAL WORLD OF SUZHOU

The second of the two most famous seminal pieces of carved lacquer was excavated from a series of family tombs not far from Shanghai which are known to date from 1338 to 1351 (Tsung, 1959). Until the discovery of this piece no one would have dared to propose so early a date for such a well-known type.

The 'Ren Tomb Box' is circular, flat-topped and relatively shallow for its surface area *(Pl. 27)*. The landscape is rimmed with a broad rouleau of simple lacquer. The bushes and trees are represented in a way we recognise as normal. At a casual glance there is little to distinguish it from a hundred other boxes. But although the type is well known it has certain individual features:

There is no building (landscapes without a pavilion are uncommon).

The profile of the rocks is markedly concave and there are none of the formally contrived holes that are usual.

The double 'edge' of the rocks is carved with a line on the inner side so that the outline is sharply distinct; the rock is 'drawn' rather than modelled in a three-dimensional way.

The diaper background, presumably from its position intended to represent air, is of the rare 'ripple' type that is recognised as an early diaper for water.

The trunk of the pine tree is marked with irregular lines running naturalistically in the direction of growth, not with a series of shallow elongated hollows or a succession of scribbles rather like punctuation marks which is more usual.

A contrivance, perhaps a stairway, appears to be lashed to the trunk of a tree.

The palings, which are evidently at two levels, are drawn as simple struts with no attempt at ornament. Between the two sets of palings there is a diaper of diamond shapes (not squares as supposed by Garner, 1979) filled with parallel lines that run in an opposite direction to its neighbour. This diaper seems to be unique.

There are no clouds.

The key-fret on the side of the box is coupled rather than running.

But these points of divergence from the norm are relatively small. What is exciting about this box is how astonishingly ordinary it seems to us, for from this box

*Plate 27 a, b **The Ren Tomb Landscape Box***

The earliest carved landscape lacquer for which there is a limiting date. It was recovered from a group of tombs near Shanghai of which the latest was datable to 1351 and the earliest to 1338. The carving is steep, the edges lightly rounded. The rocks have a concave outline which is emphasised by a raised edge. What seems to be a stairway on the right is clumsily handled: the diamond-shaped diaper between the struts makes no sense. The ties that secure the stairway to the tree suggest that 'Tao Yuanming and Attendant Picking Herbs' is the scene represented (Krahl and Morgan, 1989). One would expect the trees and bushes to be outlined against the sky but a ripple diaper is used which in other, probably later, pieces stands for water. There are no clouds. The key-fret border is coupled and not running as is usual in later Ming and Qing pieces. Yuan. Diameter 21.1 cm, depth 3.9 cm.
Shanghai Museum

derive the landscape boxes and dishes that have been made throughout six centuries.

Early landscapes have much the same ingredients: rocks, trees, pools of water, and garden pavilions in which figures are to be seen seated at a table as other figures approach or depart or stand gazing at a prospect. The distance is generally edged with rocky islets and formal clouds ride overhead. We are in a garden open to the lightest of airs. A servant brings wine. Scholars are rapt by the beauty of a waterfall. Poets observe the moon. Philosophers dispute. Guests are greeted or depart. A meal is being prepared.

It may be that these scenes illustrate some event, legendary or historical, that was part of the furniture of the cultivated Chinese gentleman of the period but is hermetic to the Western mind. Such landscapes are witness to the civilised quietism of the intelligentsia of the Song and the Yuan (*Pls. 28–31*).

The Sinan Potiche can be traced by way of ceramic moulds to embroidered silks but the Ren Tomb Box has no such antecedents. Its likely source is in painting; it is, after all, a picture in relief.

To the average educated Westerner who has no specialised knowledge of Far Eastern painting the typical Chinese landscape is a vertical scroll with mountain rising upon mountain, mist-shrouded, strange, and in the foreground, squeezed in near the foot of the scroll, the tiny figure of a man, a philosopher, mendicant, traveller, poet, significant only because he gives scale to the vastness of nature that is the real subject of the picture. But there are types of painting less familiar. There is

the horizontal scroll that can be unrolled and viewed progressively like a film strip. This may represent a panorama of mountains in which man is indeed small but no longer dominated by his background. Or the artist may concentrate on the foreground: life on a river with men fishing from their long, elegant boats, birds flying overhead. The subject is no longer the overwhelming cosmos but is still man in relation to nature not man in a building or a street. Then there are album and fan paintings, something akin to the 'cabinet' pictures of the West, which attempt within a small compass to isolate one aspect of a scene — interiors, or delightful intimate landscapes, or lakes rich in fish, fowl and flowers but without buildings or people — and among these is a small group of garden scenes such as we have in the Ren Tomb Box and in a hundred other Ming lacquer dishes and boxes. The source of these scenes in which man is shown in pseudo-natural surroundings of his own contriving appears to have been the Imperial Painting Academy in Hangzhou, which flourished in the thirteenth century.

Among the many flourishing cities of the Yangtze basin, of which Hangzhou was one, is the city of Suzhou. It is close to Lake Tai some fifty miles west of Shanghai. It had been the capital of the kingdom of Wu in the fifth century BC. It is set in fertile country with ample water, good alluvial soil and a mild climate. In this favoured spot there has long existed a leisured world, a place of retirement from officialdom, a paradise for the arts of luxury, where jade and ivory carving and embroidery flourished. It was a place particularly famed for its gardens. Was it the influence of Suzhou and neighbouring cities that created these lacquer gardenscapes?

*Plate 29 **Octagonal Dish: Sage Looking at Waterfall***

The landscape is contained in a narrow grooved rouleau. Outside this is a band of flowers and leaves set against a buff ground and framed by a larger rouleau which is grooved on the inner and outer sides. The carving is deep, well-rounded and bold. As in the Ren Tomb Box, there are no clouds and the rocks have a concave outline which is not reinforced with a raised ridge as in the box. A diaper of a double diamond enclosing a formalised floret is used to represent the land, which is separated from the water by a fairly elaborate garden fence. The ripple diaper beyond the fence clearly represents water, and waves are shown breaking about the rock at the base of the waterfall — a feature that persisted sporadically for four centuries but became conspicuous in mid-Qing. There is no dividing line between the wave diaper and the six/four cloud pattern, which here represents air. The piece is signed by Yang Mao. Yuan. Diameter 17.8 cm, depth 2.6 cm.
Palace Museum, Beijing

Plate 30 **Oval Tray**
Closely paralleled by the tray in Krahl and Morgan (1989: Pl. 8),
but lacking the floret edge. Fourteenth-century. Length 23.4 cm,
width 16.1 cm.
Los Angeles County Museum of Art

Plate 31 **Six-lobed Dish**
'Zhang Cheng' is inscribed on the base, together with a poem. An
early date, fourteenth-century, is suggested by the wide spacing of
the flowers and leaves in the cavetto and by the flat rather than
cupped treatment of the plum blossoms. The diamond rather than
square ground-diaper is usually early; the air diaper is of the
four/six pattern; the reverse of the cavetto is a classic scroll. There
are many examples of the distinctive floral rim. Although signatures are of doubtful authenticity, it is probable that all of this type
were made in a workshop in or near Suzhou. Fourteenth-century.
Diameter 16.7 cm.
Bluett & Sons Ltd.

The year in which Hongwu, the founder of the Ming
dynasty, assumed the imperial title, 1368, is also taken
to mark the end of the Yuan, but in fact disintegration
of the Mongol dynasty had been going on for at least
thirty years. A man who claimed to be a descendant of
the Song rebelled in 1350, proclaimed himself emperor
five years later and maintained a limited and unstable
local authority for eleven years. Other rebellions followed in quick succession. It was a time of troubles. A
cloth pedlar who called himself emperor established his
capital at Hanyang. A salt smuggler and pirate took
control of the Zhejiang coast. A well-to-do fortune-teller
raised the standard of rebellion and occupied
Haozhou. These were some of the more picturesque attempts, there were many others, among which the most
successful was that of Zhang Shicheng, who assumed
the title of Prince of Wu and set himself up at Suzhou.
It was during this period of political instability that the
Ren Box was made.

Changes of political control often cause scarcely a ripple in well-established communities. Not only in China

Plate 32 **Lobed Red Dish**

This landscape without figures is linked to the mid-fourteenth century by the floret edge and the diamond-shaped earth-diaper, although the water diaper undulates rather than ripples. Its lobed outline and ridged inner frame relate it to the great polychrome dish in the British Museum *(Pl. 39)* and a more usual landscape dish in the Victoria and Albert Museum (Strange, 1925: Pl. 22). In all three, and in the floret-edged dishes in plate 31 and in Krahl and Morgan (1989: Pl. 8), the floral border is similar. Although in San Francisco it is called late fifteenth-century (1985), the evidence points to the mid-fourteenth. Yuan. Diameter 31 cm, depth 3.8 cm.
Avery Brundage Collection, Asian Art Museum of San Francisco

Plate 33 **Box**
Garner discusses this box (1973) and compares it with a nearly
identical landscape dish in the Low Beer collection in which, how-
ever, the rock modelling is in the strongly contoured style of
Yunnan. Yongle. Diameter 26.6 cm.
Freer Gallery of Art, Washington, DC

Plate 34 **Large Daoist Box**
Brown-black lacquer interior and base. Figures are posed dramatically and expressively; hands and feet are shown. The elaboration of its staffage is an exception to the official landscapes of early Ming which this otherwise resembles. It should therefore be early (before conformity was imposed) or late (when conformity began to relax) or an exceptional order for a specific Daoist purpose. It relates to a box in Beijing called Xuande (Palace Museum, 1985: Pl. 99) that is red on green. Yongle. Diameter 31 cm, depth 9.5 cm.
Aberdeen City Art Gallery

but throughout the world the trumpetings of warlords do not immediately disturb the lives of ordinary citizens. The elegant, studious, intellectual, epicurean life of Suzhou continued with little change. Zhang was an intelligent prince who provided a congenial atmosphere for literary men, but when in the autumn of 1367 he was defeated by a rival prince, later to be the

Hongwu Emperor, the victor almost immediately began the removal of the rich families from the city, transferring them to his own capital at Nanjing. The departure of their patrons must have had a severe effect on the artisans of Suzhou and it is likely that many followed their clients to Nanjing.

But Suzhou did not change permanently. It remained as it is today a city of gardens. Those strange, enclosed worlds of pavilions, water and rocks endured throughout the Ming and Qing dynasties and still exist today, repaired, restored and reconstructed throughout the centuries but still essentially places for studious retirement and civilised enjoyment of the subtle pleasures of life. The spiritual home and probably the physical origins of the familiar type of carved lacquer are to be found in this favoured neighbourhood.

CHAPTER 6

DIAPERS AND GUIDELINES

The first Ming emperor, Hongwu, an auto-didact, a former Buddhist monk and one who paid lip-service to Confucianism, was a military conqueror, a great organiser of the empire, the author of many books, an imitator of history and a respecter of tradition. During his reign, that of his grandson Jianwen and the greater part of the reign of his son, Yongle, the capital of the Ming was Nanjing and the culture of the lower Yangtze valley became the culture of the court. Although lacquer was made in many other centres, the Ren Tomb Box and the Sinan Potiche are central to the development of mainstream lacquer.

The divergence of ancestry between these two important pieces is apparent in the handling of the background. The background of the Ren Box is carved with formal waves or ripples but the background of the floral Potiche is plain yellow or buff. When the two subjects are brought together on the same piece the custom persists, the landscapes are closely carved with a pattern of various diapers in red whereas the floral borders stand against uncarved yellow. This argues a marriage of traditions.

Designs of the guri type do not have a background and some early flower-and-bird dishes are so close-knit that the depth of the cut appears as little more than a dark

linear shadow and there is virtually no background visible. Later, as the pattern became more open again, leaving a space between its components, there arose the problem of what to do with the space. It was no longer felt satisfactory to leave it blank as in the Boston tray (Boston Museum of Fine Arts, 1982) or that in the Tokyo National Museum (1989: Pl. 197).

As fourteenth- and early fifteenth-century floral pieces were essentially not pictures but patterns that derived from ceramic moulds and embroideries, at first it seemed sufficient to use as a background a different colour, yellow or buff, which could be held to replace the gold in silks in order to make the pattern more positive. Because landscapes, on the other hand, were pictures rather than patterns, illusion required that the spaces between the features be accepted as earth, water or air. Consequently appropriate symbolic conventions were established in the form of diapers.

The most thorough enquiry into the geometry of diapers was made by Sir Harry Garner in his article 'Diaper Backgrounds on Chinese Carved Lacquer' (Garner, 1966). The article is too long to summarise here but those who wish to go into the subject more fully should refer to it. But even Garner fails to exhaust the subject.

The background of the Ren Box is covered with the
rare 'ripple' diaper. It is just possible that Garner who
christened this diaper 'ripple' may have got it wrong,
for in the Ren Box it can be read as air not as water,
and the ripple may first have been conceived as clouds
rather than waves. However, in support of Garner is the
fact that in four out of the five pieces that have the ripple it is used in association with other conventions that
clearly stand for land and air so that no room is left for
doubt.

The ripple diaper appears not to have been used for
long but was replaced by the wave diaper, in which a
succession of roughly triangular forms represent the
undulation of water. In the Nezu Art Gallery of Japan is
a circular box with a scratched Yongle reign mark on
the base that uses both forms, the 'ripple' perhaps intended for shore waters and the 'wave' for open sea. It
was perhaps made at the point of transition. The box
may indeed be Yongle, as the floral sides suggest, but is
probably earlier and can with reasonable confidence be
ascribed to the reign of Hongwu. The wave diaper is
more easily carved than the ripple and although at first
it was drawn with some freedom, it was soon constructed on a repetitive geometric plan.

The standard air diaper, which Garner traced with great
precision, is an evolution of the ripple. What he described as a succession of 'stars' is formed by the cross-
ing of lines in such a way that the neighbouring stars,
the points of intersection, are not on the same horizontal, the star on the left being two bars higher than the
star on the right. This Garner called the 'six/four' pattern. The reverse, in which the star on the right is the
higher, he called the 'four/six', which he reasonably
supposed was a variant arrived at by using the pattern
guide the other way round. The next stage, the 'parallel' air diaper, is a development of lines so that the stars
appear on a level with their neighbours. Finally, by the
reign of Jiajing, the diaper is sometimes already reduced to a succession of disconnected rectangles (Low
Beer, 1952: Pls. 50, 51).

Land diapers appear variously as small squares, diamond shapes, hexagons, circles or complex combina-
tions of all these, filled with formalised flowers.

Diamonds are common in early pieces but there seems
to be no rule governing their use. Delicate, complicated encircled hexagons and like patterns are usually
limited to small boxes, appearing first in the fifteenth
century and thereafter with increasing frequency until
the nineteenth.

The limited way in which they are used on the Ren Box
implies that the convention of appropriate diapers was
not yet fully established in the second quarter of the
fourteenth century. Most early and mid-fifteenth-century pieces use the forms of diaper proper to land,
water and air, and do not confuse them, but by the sixteenth century they are not always used in a meaningful
way. As always when trying to establish firm rules in
Chinese art, one is tripped up by exceptions: a particularly fine Yongle/Xuande box in Beijing closely carved
with two five-clawed dragons amongst peonies has a
background of square diapers that is decorative rather
than symbolic *(Pl. 35)*. As patterns opened out and the
ideal of very close carving was abandoned, which had
happened by the second decade of the fifteenth century, it became more than ever necessary to replace the
simple yellow ground with a carved one.

There are very few examples of Yuan/early Ming landscapes with a key-fret as in the Ren Box and it is generally safe to conclude that those that have it date from
about the same time. It is usual for boxes, whether the
tops are carved with a landscape or with a bird-and-
flower design, to have a band of flowers, usually 'the
flowers of the four seasons', around the side and these
invariably have a yellow ground. On dishes however,
whether the main subject is landscape or flowers, the
equivalent of the sides of boxes, the reverse of the
cavetto, has the trailing guri-type design of the classic
scroll, whose presence is a fair indication that the piece
is fourteenth-century.

The lacquer body of the later fourteenth-century wares
is generally, but not always, made up in the same way.
First, a composition layer was applied to the foundation
and this was followed by a few layers of yellow, then by a
rather greater thickness of red, followed by a thin line
of black, and upon that base was applied a final and
much greater thickness of red. The yellow or buff layer
was there to provide a background for the flower and
flower-and-bird dishes, but was not required for landscapes. As the majority of landscape pieces, whether
boxes or dishes, were bordered or edged with a band of
flowers, the whole lacquer body had to be treated in the
same way. For the carver of flower patterns there was
no difficulty: he worked until he reached the yellow
and then stopped. But when carving landscapes he had
to avoid breaking through to the depth of the yellow

which was why the thin layer of black was inserted as a warning to him to stop. Black pieces that were to have a yellow ground had no need of a guideline, the carver stopped when the yellow showed, but in those that did not have a contrasted ground the black was applied above the composition base and a red line was inserted above that as a warning. Plate 6 shows the damaged corner of the guri vase-stand in plate 5, in which the red guideline is clearly visible.

The presence of a simple guideline can be taken as evidence of a fourteenth- or fifteenth-century date, but its absence does not prove the contrary. For example, the Ren Box has no black guideline although there do appear to be two distinct tones of red. And it is clear that the orange tone of the earliest landscapes (*Pls. 11, 12*) is caused by the carver having broken through to the yellow ground. Probably the true narrow guideline was used, and then not invariably, only in the early fifteenth century, because when a base colour differed from the surface colour the guideline became superfluous as such, although it may have been retained briefly as an aid to fracture (*Pl. 52*).

It is necessary at this point to run ahead of historical development so that the subject of the guideline may be followed through. Before long it became apparent that what had started as a simple device to aid the carver could be developed into an economic advantage. By substituting a thick layer of bastard lacquer in place of the guideline, the number of layers of pure lacquer needed was reduced and so was the time needed to prepare it. The often-repeated statement that 100 or 200 layers of lacquer, each involving several days' setting time, were necessary for really fine work, is untrue. Gao Lian, in *Eight Discourses on the Art of Living* (1591), asserted that in the reign of Yongle a court edict ordered that thirty-six layers must be used.

Garner dismissed this by saying that even a moderate piece could not be produced in so shallow a body (1979); but if a certain amount of adulterated lacquer was used in the middle, as a sort of sandwich filling between the surface and the base level, thirty-six coats may well have been enough. Some early pieces that have been tested do indeed have 100 or 200 coats, but others do not. The deeply carved pieces of the eighteenth century (*Pl. 103*) can only be explained if we accept that an adulterated lacquer had been evolved that set quickly in much thicker layers than pure lacquer. Such an 'extended guideline' was already in use by the fifteenth century and probably earlier; it is certainly present in the Xuande-marked box-lid in plate 47, in the box-lid in plate 57 and in the tiered box in the Victoria and Albert Museum that was in Garner's collection (Garner, 1973 b: No. 79). It is clear from this last example and from the box in plate 42 that a diluted lacquer was used for the carved body and that several layers of more brightly coloured pure lacquer were painted over the top. In the case of the last two boxes, the final coat was a later addition and is so thin that it is beginning to wear through. There is nothing remarkable about this use of adulterated lacquer for, in one form or another, it had been used many centuries before in moulded pieces. It was the brief period when only pure lacquer was used that is remarkable.

Yellow or buff grounds are not in themselves a guarantee of earliness for they can be found on sixteenth-century pieces and even, though rarely, on examples as late as mid-Qing. Early yellow grounds nearly always show a tendency to flake whereas late fifteenth-century examples do not (*Pl. 9*).

By the mid-fifteenth century a great deal of lacquer was made in two shades of red. The main body was darker and duller than the surface, possibly due to a greater mixture of tong oil, and above the dull red there was another lighter level. There is no consistency of practice. When polychrome lacquer became popular, as it did in the late sixteenth century, a guideline was unnecessary and the position had virtually returned to that of the fourteenth-century guri lacquers. By the time of Qianlong the lacquer-masters had learned to control the depth of carving so that no guideline was necessary even when one tone of bright red lacquer was used throughout (*Pl. 107*).

CHAPTER 7

MARKS OF YONGLE AND XUANDE

One of the many gaps in our knowledge relates to those lacquers dated between 1351 (The Ren Tomb Box) and the reign of Yongle (1403–24). We know that in 1403 a gift of carved lacquer was sent by Yongle to the shogun in Japan (Figgess, 1962–63). As these would have taken perhaps as long as two years to make, it must be assumed that they were made in the brief reign of Yongle's nephew, Jianwen, or of his father, Hongwu. It has become the custom to attribute early examples of the main tradition either to the Yuan dynasty or to Yongle, tacitly ignoring the certainty that many of them were made under the first two Ming emperors. A judgement as to which pieces are Yuan, which Hongwu, or Jianwen, or Yongle, has to be largely subjective. There is however a certain amount of circumstantial evidence upon which, lacking any other, we can build.

In the Palace Museum in Beijing is preserved a huge hoard of lacquer which must be the accumulation of pieces made for the court after the date of its transference to the Forbidden City from Nanjing. The transfer to the north took place in 1421 and it is reasonable to suppose that the court brought with them some of the lacquer that had been in the palace at Nanjing. There is likely to have been very little dating from before 1402, for in that year the usurping Yongle captured the city and Jianwen's palace was burned down and his empress and child perished. It follows that by far the greater number of early pieces in the Palace hoard will be of the Yongle period. Nevertheless, there are ten pieces in the collection that are considered by the authorities there to be either Yuan or early Ming, in other words pre-Yongle, and there is supporting evidence for their opinion.

Four of these early pieces are signed by an artist. Despite the teamwork nature of lacquer production, it is evident that credit for the work was sometimes given to the carver. There is a dish carved boldly with a pattern of gardenias which is signed by Zhang Cheng (Pl. 23); a flowerpot, already referred to, with an everted lip is signed by Yang Mao (Pl. 18); an octagonal dish with a landscape within a floral border is signed by the same man (Pl. 29); and a circular box with a floral side is signed by Zhang Minde. It is customary for the cautious to doubt the signatures of the first two because they are mentioned by name in the Ge Gu Yao Lun and, the reference being well-known, some signatures will undoubtedly have been faked — but surely not within the imperial collection? Their work was held in high repute at the time but was said to be marred by being rather thin and fragile, although it is not absolutely clear whether this referred to their work or to that of their contemporaries.

Apart from their evident fame in 1388 their dates are confirmed by the fact that when the Yongle Emperor heard of them in the middle years of his reign and sent for them, both men were dead. In default, Zhang Cheng's son, Zhang Degang, was appointed assistant director in charge of the production of lacquer in the government factory. Nothing is known of Zhang Minde but the bowl he signed looks to be later than the others (Palace Museum, 1985: Pl. 5).

The two pieces signed by Yang Mao, the flowerpot and the octagonal landscape, despite the difference of subject, could well be by the same hand and they illustrate the coming together of the two strands of early carved lacquer, the flowers of the Sinan Potiche and the landscape of the Ren Box. The dish is in some ways the more interesting because not only is the landscape related to the Ren Box through the concave outline of its rocks but also the broad edge of flowers that surrounds it is carved in the same manner as the potiche and the flowerpot. It is to the flowerpot in Beijing that the necked bottle in the BASF Lacquer Museum in Munster *(Pl. 19)*, its near pair in Taiwan (National Palace Museum, 1987: Pl. 6) and the bamboo-necked bottle in the British Museum *(Pl. 20)* are related. There is yet another flowerpot in Beijing (Palace Museum, 1985: Pl. 46), similar to the first but bearing a long inscription added to the base by Qianlong. It is said there to be Yongle but the rim of the foot is carved with a coupled key-fret as in the Ren Box and it has a good chance of being a Yuan piece. In the Victoria and Albert Museum there is a domed incense box that Garner illustrated and unaccountably called 'sixteenth-to seventeenth-century' (Garner, 1979) . It bears the same signature as the flowerpot and is from the same workshop. Added indication of an early date is the coupled rather than running key-fret around the foot rim.

There are forty-two pieces in the Beijing catalogue attributed to the reign of Yongle: sixteen of them are landscapes but there are a fair number of flower pieces. All this lacquer, produced — as we must assume — by order of the court during the Yongle period, shows a certain standardised excellence.

There are no reign-marked pieces of Hongwu, the first Ming emperor, but there are several Yongle ones.

Yongle marks are incised with a needle and Xuande marks are cut with a knife and filled in with gold. On a number of pieces both marks occur, sometimes with the Xuande mark superimposed over the Yongle. There are several explanations for this overmarking. The most probable is that there were considerable stocks when Yongle died, and that rather than discard them, the economically minded eunuch in charge caused the mark to be changed. There is another explanation: that some later enthusiastic connoisseur, emperor or factory overseer, going through the earlier and more interesting part of the collection marked the pieces as he thought appropriate and that a still later 'expert', disagreeing, re-marked them.

If we could be sure that the Xuande marks were placed over the Yongle because the pieces were already in the factory store when the emperor died, we should have no difficulty in identifying a late Yongle style. Because this is uncertain, we must suppose that in the sixteenth century (when it is alleged that the greater number of these marks were made) knowledgeable people differed as to which side of 1424 such pieces should be attributed. We may take this as evidence that doubly marked pieces are in fact late Yongle. Garner thought that all the Yongle and most of the Xuande marks were made in the sixteenth century, but if so why were they written differently? It is likely that if they were late additions the inscriber will have marked them as he did because he knew that authentic Yongle and Xuande marks were applied in different ways. Surely then it is not improbable that some genuine marks still existed?

There are two possible ways to determine whether a piece was made in the reign of Yongle. The first is to accept those that bear his scratched reign mark on the left of the base or, since the mark does sometimes appear on pieces that are doubtfully of that time, only to accept those that form a coherent corpus. The second way would be to identify those pieces that were sent to Japan between 1403 and 1424 and to accept that the common denominator constitutes a genuine 'Yongle' style. This, it seems, we cannot do and are therefore thrown back on accepting marked pieces in the Palace collection that appear on stylistic grounds to be about right and to call these and such others as we can relate to them 'Yongle'. And this, in fact, is what is done and will continue to be done until convincing contrary evidence is found.

CHAPTER 8

OFFICIAL WARE AND THE PALACE COLLECTION AT BEIJING

At some time early in the fifteenth century, or late in the fourteenth, the production of lacquer for the imperial court was concentrated in the hands of a government-controlled factory, resulting in the production of what Garner and Low Beer called 'official' ware. That such a source of lacquer production existed no one who has studied lacquer can doubt, but the certainty with which some pieces are attributed to the official factory and others are excluded is open to question. The fact is there were many centres of lacquer production supplying a variety of markets in widely separated areas and working in various manners and producing work of variable quality. We know very little of these factories. Some no doubt will have emulated the court style and possibly produced work of equal or greater merit; others will have developed their own idiosyncrasies, or under commercial pressure have worked to lower standards.

The mark of 'official' ware is extreme technical skill. Whatever the overseers of the imperial factories succeeded in doing by way of regimenting individual vision and genius, they sought to make up for it by insistence on an extraordinary degree of exactitude, conformity and high finish. These are the qualities that Garner and Low Beer elevated above all others. The official ware of the Yongle period conforms not only to certain standards of technical excellence but also to a depressingly consistent repetition of accepted forms.

The basis of the official style was a combination of the Ren Box and the Sinan Potiche and once these had synthesised into an acceptable form, there for a generation it stayed. The characteristic shape of Yongle lacquer was the shallow straight-sided box with a landscape or floral lid and sides of close-packed flowers of the four seasons (Pl. 33).

In the Palace collection at Beijing are eighteen landscapes that are regarded as pre-Xuande and since it is unlikely that many were Yuan the majority may be thought of as Hongwu or Yongle. Eight of these landscapes are on dishes and ten are on boxes. Of the dishes one is octagonal, one is square and lobed, another is square with indented corners, one is simply circular and the remaining four are circular and multilobed. Most have a broad border of leaves and flowers showing a marriage of themes of the Sinan Potiche and the Ren Box. All but one are framed with a broad rouleau; the exception, with a grooved rouleau, is a circular dish. All but two of the boxes are straight-sided, the remaining two are deeper and slope to the side and again inward at the bottom towards a narrow key-fret foot rim. None of the boxes are decorated on the sides with the coupled key-fret as the Ren Box is.

Plate 36 **Five-tiered Box on Stand**
At the top is a landscape with a figure in a pavilion approached by
a servant bringing wine; another figure is on the shore by a lotus
pool. A nest with young birds is in the water. There are good foliage edges as in the Victoria and Albert table *(Pl. 44)*. The decoration on the flanged foot rim is a cut form of classic scroll. Land is
shown by two-level carving with a linear edge; rocks as in 'The
Necromancer' *(Pl. 66)*; there is a high finish. Similar tiered boxes
in Beijing are called Xuande. Xuande. Height 14.7 cm, maximum
width 11.7 cm, depth 11.5 cm.
Aberdeen City Art Gallery

Despite these variations there is a sameness about all
these pieces. The floral bands are all much alike, flowers of the Potiche type have been accommodated to a
ribbon shape. Sometimes there are repetitions and variations of one formal flower, but more often the pattern
is based on the flowers of the four seasons: peony,
pomegranate, chrysanthemum and camellia. The gardenscapes echo one another. They are the Ren Box
with additions: there is a pavilion within which figures
are visible, seated at a table or by an open lattice win-
dow; a garden fence, more or less elaborate, divides the
middle distance; a pine tree, gnarled and picturesquely
twisted, leans out from behind the pavilion; a figure,
perhaps two, sometimes more, walks in the garden; visi-
tors are greeted. The whole is irregularly framed with

decorative rocks and bushes of indeterminate species,
the distance is occupied by the waters of a lake into
which jut the noses of headlands and islands. Overhead
are clouds of irredeemable solidity. The pieces are
moved about in an effort to produce variety, the pavilion is now to the left, now to the right, the pine tree is
replaced by a pendulous willow, the pavilion becomes
more complicated, rising in several tiers like a wedding
cake, sometimes it develops into a range of buildings,
the leaves of a giant plantain add an exotic note, and a
bird flies over. And usually that is all. The craftsmanship
is excellent but the distances are not exploited and the
imposed shape of dish or box-lid and the prescribed ingredients give little scope for variety so that designs
seem crowded and airless.

Contemporary with these gardenscapes are pieces entirely decorated with flowers in the manner of the
Sinan Potiche. Some are of the shallow box type but
with flowers instead of a landscape on the top; many
more are dishes of a simple circular unlobed form.
Rarely, they incorporate amongst the flowers a dragon
or a phoenix, emblematic of emperor and empress.

There is no comparable collection with so many late
fourteenth- and early fifteenth-century pieces. What
general conclusions can we draw from it as to the character of the court's 'official' taste of the period? The
fifty-five pieces, all red, break down like this:

Landscape as the principal feature		18
Flowers as the principal feature		26
Flowers in conjunction with dragons or other beasts		5
Flowers with birds		3
Guri patterns		3
Boxes		32
Box, circular with rounded edge and straight sides	2	
Box, rectangular	1	
Box, flattened circle	2	
Box, deep circular	26	
Box, deep octagonal, segmented sides	1	
Dishes		17
Jar shape		2
Lidded bowl		1
Bowl-stand		2
Low table		1

Allowing for the fact that some of these pieces are possibly wrongly attributed to the Hongwu/Yongle period,
and accepting that the group is in fact representative of
court taste, we can say that guri (three only) pieces

Plate 37 **Hexagonal Four-tiered Box**

The top is carved at two levels but the figures are largely proud of the upper surface and are deeply undercut to accentuate the three-dimensional appearance. A rotund god is seated on a fringed mat of very fine diamond diapers. The ground is represented by delicate florets and the water by freely drawn waves. There are no clouds and rocks. The pine trunk leans from the frame and its branches return in the upper right corner. Garner attributed a rectangular box of this type to the late fifteenth century despite a Zhang Cheng signature (Garner, 1979), whereas Beijing illustrates three as Xuande (Palace Museum, 1985). Tiered boxes were in-cluded in the gift of lacquer sent to the shogun in 1403 and these must have been made in the fourteenth century. It is probable that the type continued in production with little variation for many years. Certainly the Beijing examples appear to be Xuande but this box, because of its freely drawn waves, the absence of rocks and clouds, and its rich colour, has a claim to be considered fourteenth-century. Nevertheless, the steep change of level, the line separating land from water and the hexagonal floret diaper, all compel an at-tribution to Xuande. Xuande. Height 13.2 cm.
Private collection

were no longer liked; that bird-and-flower were not as popular as they had been under the Yuan; that black as an overall colour was 'out'; that boxes and dishes make up the majority of pieces; and that basic shapes tended to be conservative.

Bearing in mind that the period covered was fifty-six years (and if some of these pieces are Yuan a great deal more) we should have expected greater variety, but Hongwu, despite Confucian beginnings, became a tyrannous monarch and savagely authoritarian, and during his reign a strongly conservative style was imposed. Yongle was also content to stabilise the institutions of his father and it is likely that some of the divergent forms, such as the lobed dishes, date from the later years of his reign and should be called Yongle/Xuande.

There are, of course, other indicators. It is fairly clear that broad simple rouleaux pre-date grooved ones since the grooved sort are more common in examples regarded as Xuande. Yellow-buff backgrounds to all flower-related pieces are so general that it is with a shock that we find a magnificent flower-and-dragon box with a standard earth diaper; it is to be presumed that it is Yongle/Xuande (*Pl. 35*).

The condition of a piece also affects one's judgement and yet this, like other guides, is not altogether reliable. It is true that Yuan wares are often warped and that Ming 'official' lacquers have for the most part overcome the technical difficulties that caused it, but there are exceptions. The circumstances in which examples were kept can result in different degrees of wear. Remarkably undamaged pieces are sometimes genuine although one would normally expect a certain amount of wear and cracking, particularly of the base. Black bases do crack although mahogany-coloured bases in natural-coloured lacquer seem not to. The bases of pieces that have been in Japan have often been relacquered. In so far as faking was done, and there are no certain examples to guide us, it has been said that the faker could simulate the cracks that appear on the base of a genuine piece as well as those deeper cracks that are often found on the edges (Lee, 1972). It is doubtful however whether it could possibly have paid the fakers who are alleged to have worked at the beginning of this century to produce work of a standard sufficiently high to deceive, particularly since there was at that time no demand for genuine Ming lacquer in the West although there may still have been in China. In earlier centuries close copying or faking may well have been common to satisfy Chinese collectors.

There remain the pieces of Hongwu/Yongle date that were not 'official'. Our best but inadequate guides are the lists of pieces recorded to have been sent by Yongle to the consort of the shogun of Japan in 1403, 1406 and 1407. These lists mention 203 pieces of carved lacquer in all, many of them described in some detail. The 1403 list contains no fewer than six large dishes with birds against a background of flowers. These are rare in the Beijing collection and we may therefore conclude that most are of the fourteenth century. On the other hand the lists refer to tiered boxes, several of which in the Beijing hoard are ascribed to Xuande but none to Yongle. The Xuande attributions are right but it is evident that tiered boxes were being made in the fourteenth century, although perhaps not by the factory that worked for the court (*Pls. 36, 37*).

Stylistically, the great difference between the Song and early Yuan flower or flower-and-bird dishes and those of Hongwu/Yongle is in the amount of background allowed to appear. In the dated Song dish in Boston, and its near pair in Tokyo, each leaf and flower and bird is set in isolation upon a yellow-buff ground. This is easy to design and to carve but involves cutting to waste a great deal of valuable lacquer. As skills increased so the amount of background diminished until in many of the early Ming examples it is as though the carver had merely outlined the features of his design and allowed no background to be visible.

CHAPTER 9

THE 'RIPPLE' WATER DIAPER

To these landscapes made at the government factory under strict supervision there are remarkable exceptions which, if they do not pre-date palace control, were certainly free of it.

Some such pieces, grouped about the Ren Box by their common use of the ripple diaper, pose problems. The nearest to the Box is an octagonal dish in Beijing *(Pl. 29)*. The simple landscape is surrounded by a floral border which is bounded by bold rouleaux. The ripple diaper represents water and the earth is shown by a diamond enclosing a formalised flower, the air by a six/four arrangement. It is easy to see from this dish how, with a little adjustment, the ripple could become a series of interlocking bolster shapes which in turn became the sky diaper. The rocks are beginning to develop holes and their outline, although concave, is no longer defined by a raised ridge as in the Ren Box and they are heavier at the edges. This dish bears the signature of the famous artist-lacquerer, Yang Mao, and may well be his work.

Another 'ripple' piece, a fine lobed dish, is illustrated by Lee Yu-kuan (1972: Pl. 101). The border is the usual flowers of the four seasons but the edge of the dish is fringed with florets in circles. There is a simple pavilion and the paling, unlike the Ren Box, is ornate. Land is represented by diamonds containing formal florets as in the Beijing example (diamond shapes rather than squares are often an indication, but not a guarantee, of earliness). There are ducks on the water. The point of change from the ripple to the four/six diaper is not at first sight clear. The leafage over the pavilion attempts to be more naturalistic than the symbolic leaves in the Ren Box and the trees try in a childlike way to represent distinct though doubtful species. It is signed by the other of the pair of famous lacquerers, Zhang Cheng. From its primitive character this dish looks near in date to the Ren Box whereas the more sophisticated Beijing dish *(Pl. 29)* should be later.

Two other dishes with the ripple diaper are unusual in being pure landscapes staffed with neither buildings or people. In the Asian Art Museum of San Francisco is a circular dish of which the edge is carved with florets in circles *(Pl. 38)* just as in the Lee Yu-kuan dish. The landscape is contained in a six-lobed frame of a broad flat ribbon of lacquer, beyond this is a border of boldly carved flowers of the four seasons. The dish itself is circular. The foreground of the landscape is of flowers, rushes, and lotus leaves growing out of the water, which spring to two-thirds of the picture height. In the sky a bird flies over and there are clouds. The water diaper, although of a ripple pattern, is unlike the others in that it is more freely drawn.

Plate 38 **Red Dish**
The ripple water-diaper links this dish with the Ren Tomb Box
(Pl. 28). A pure landscape is contained within a six-lobed border
which in turn is bordered with flowers of the four seasons inside a
floret-edged circle. It is called fifteenth-century, but the ripple dia-
per is a strong pointer to a mid-fourteenth-century date. Yuan.
Diameter 23, height 3.4 cm.
Avery Brundage Collection, Asian Art Museum of San Francisco

Plate 39 **Lobed Dish**
A pure landscape with the early ripple form of water-diaper not
clearly differentiated from the air-diaper. The reverse of the cavetto
has a classic scroll border. Its Engakuji provenance argues for an
early fourteenth-century date. Yuan. Diameter 43 cm.
British Museum

A lobed dish with nine brackets in the British Museum has a ripple pattern that seems to extend into the sky (*Pl. 39*). Alone of this group it is polychrome, black and red, with a border of flowers black against a yellow ground. Ducks float on the water and clouds squeeze in at the top. There is no land diaper because the scene has been given a natural foreground of rocks and flowers, and the adventure into naturalism extends to the trees on either side. A pair of birds perch on a projecting branch. It is pure landscape untrampled by man. Garner hesitantly dated this to the fourteenth or fifteenth century, but the ripple brings it down on the earlier date.

A fifth is the large seven-lobed 'Kindergarten Dish' (*Pl. 40*). A pavilion less elaborate than usual and half-hidden by the hanging branches of a willow stands on struts above a lotus pool in which birds float. It is at an angle to the spectator. There is a well-designed fence about the pool and a large specimen rock is mounted within a box in a corner of the garden. There is a sense of spaciousness here that is lacking in the official landscapes. The trick of hanging willow branches from beyond the picture space, combined with the diagonals of the pavilion, takes the eye into a convincing distance. The refreshing naturalism is exuberantly continued in the human scene. Two elegant ladies supervise what must be a nursery school, one holds a child in her arms, the other, seated, has a child in her lap. Two children play on the veranda of the pavilion, one has climbed the protective balustrade and is edging around above the water. In the remaining space children crawl, tumble, wave flags, struggle with umbrellas, are bathed, squabble, play blindman's-buff, ride hobby horses and hide in the hollows of the rock. It is utterly charming and far removed from the standard garden type. Clearly, it is the work of an individual, a sophisticated and observant artist, rather than of a well-disciplined team of craftsmen working on a production line.

Another exceptional piece is in Munster (*Pl. 41*). There is the usual pavilion in the usual place, in it is seated a sage behind whom stands a servant, before the pavilion is a pool in which the lotuses are in bloom, beyond are the waters of some great lake into which a promontory protrudes. Above the pavilion rises a willow of which the tresses move gracefully in a slight breeze. Yet despite the breeze there is a stillness, the stillness of contemplation, and there is air above the lotus pool and distance beyond the willow. The delicacy, the mood, of this landscape, its use of space, are the work of an individual mind and hand. A distinctive feature is the foliate rouleau of the picture's inner frame. A similar but not identical inner frame is on a deep box at Beijing

called Yongle. Other examples of this type of frame are an attractive tray in Los Angeles that is called Yuan (*Pl. 30*) and three others, all called fourteenth-century, shown by Bluett & Sons in 1989 (Krahl and Morgan, 1989: Nos. 8, 9 & 10).

Yet another 'ripple' piece was in the Figgess collection (Christie's, December 1983, Lot 49) but this is a polychrome piece which is difficult to accommodate with an early date. Although called Yuan/Ming, its colours — red, black, green and yellow-brown — suggest a Xuande date at the earliest. Nevertheless, if the appearance of green in Yuan carved lacquer can be established then this singular piece will fit into place.

Among these unofficial wares there are contradictory indicators. Are we laying too much emphasis on their common use of the ripple diaper? Are they all of the fourteenth century, before the Ming imposed the uniform technical excellence that Garner and the others have so much admired? Without the presence of the ripple it might have been difficult to think so. An attractive interpretation is that the ripple was used over a somewhat longer period by a small and individual atelier.

About the mid-fourteenth century the ripple seems to have been replaced by undulating waves. This, the commonest water diaper, appears quite early, certainly on Yongle pieces. Variants are likely to have been the work of provincial factories not working for the court. On some the water is shown by waves not perfectly regular but freely drawn, on others these graceful curves become exaggerated humps. More elaborate wave patterns appear rarely in Xuande pieces, but by the time of Wanli crested and tumbling waves squeeze into the im-

Plate 40 **The Kindergarten Dish**
This is one of the most individual and beautiful landscape dishes in existence. It shows a complex scene within a flat-lobed frame beyond which is an open-spaced floral band bounded by a simple rouleau. The diaper representing the garden within which the children play is a double square set diagonally, each centred with a formalised floret. The diaper of the lotus pool where ducks float is a freely drawn variant of the ripple design. There is no natural physical feature to divide the water from the air diaper; a deeply engraved line inadequately marks the change from water to four/six cloud pattern. The rocks, pitted with holes, have no defining ridges. A large specimen rock is mounted in the garden. The bark of the tree is indicated by continuous lines in the direction of growth. Two women supervise the activities of a scattering of children. It is a scene of great humanity and humour, unequalled in carved lacquer of any period. The carving is flat-surfaced with abrupt rounded edges. Although sharing features with the Ren Tomb Box this is of a different nature, the work of a painter rather than a carver. Its natural, relaxed and elegiac quality is echoed in plate 42. Yuan. Diameter 55.5 cm.
Spink & Son Ltd

Plate 41 *The Lotus Pool Dish*

The landscape is said to be of Zhou Dunyi contemplating the lotus (Strasser, 1988). Beyond the flat narrow bracket frame is a border of flowers of the four seasons. The dish is framed with a narrow rouleau; the reverse of the cavetto has a spiral scroll. There is a black guideline. Yuan. Diameter 32.2 cm, depth 3.5 cm.
BASF Lacquer Museum, Munster

Plate 42 a, b *The Masquerade Box*

A scene of children masquerading is on the lid, and an extensive horizontal landscape is on the sides of the box. The original colour was red but for some inscrutable reason it was relacquered with a black coat and subsequently covered with vermilion paint which on the lid turned to a typical late seventeenth-century brown red and wore through to expose the black beneath. These extraordinary proceedings are not without precedent. The base and inside have a thin coat of translucent mahogany-coloured lacquer through which the grain of the wooden body is visible. Zhengtong/Jingtai or earlier. Diameter 6.5 cm, depth 3.2 cm.
Private collection

Plate 43 *Red Box*

The coupled key-fret might suggest an earlier date were it not that the running form is more difficult to achieve on small boxes. Early fifteenth-century. Diameter 6.4 cm.
Rijksmuseum, Amsterdam

mediate foreground and resolve into the common undulating pattern in the middle distance. During the early Qing these bravura waters became very fashionable and occupied the entire carved surface from which dragons and sea-beasts emerged disporting themselves *(Pl. 105)*. In the meantime, the undulating wave continued to be used and eventually became degraded into a form constructed on a system of intersecting diagonals that is almost always the mark of the nineteenth and twentieth centuries.

Although there is good reason for supposing that the ripple diaper is fourteenth-century, that other distinctive feature of the Ren Box, the coupled key-fret that decorates the side, is a less certain guide. The running key-fret occurs throughout the fifteenth century and is usual right through to the Qing and up to the present day. Had it not been for the excavated box there would have been a tendency to regard key-fret in any form as likely to be late. The box from the Ren family tomb has changed all that. Lee Yu-kuan illustrates a box shallow in proportion to its surface with a coupled key-fret side (Lee, 1964: Pl. 14). The scene is simple: there are some clouds of a slightly eccentric shape, but there is no building. The carving is of the rounded soft-edged type throughout. The land diaper is square, the sky is standard six/four. The bark on the tree is shown by sharp jabs of the carving tool; there is no general attempt at naturalism. On the bottom is a mark that reads 'Zhang

Cheng zao'. It could be by the same hand as plate 23. Yet another box (Lee, 1964: Pl. 33) has a design of peonies on the top and a double key-fret on the side. In both boxes the key-fret is paired but the raised lines of the key-fret are bold and single in the floral piece and are ridged in the landscape, as they are in the Ren Box. Does this mean that the floral box is the earlier? It is likely.

There are other coupled-fret boxes about which one is less sure. A small box (Lee, 1964: Pl. 23), hexagonal with a single figure against a diaper of sky, is difficult to date but may be fourteenth-century. One need have less doubt about the engaging six-lobed box in the Rijksmuseum, Amsterdam (Pl. 43). It has the four/six sky, a squared floret for land and a reasonable attempt at realism in the tumbling waterfall. Another small box in the British Museum has a good claim to be of Yuan date on stylistic grounds (Pl. 28).

What makes one sometimes hesitate overdating the coupled key-fret is that many small boxes in the National Palace Museum at Taibei have similar sides. Can they all be fourteenth-century or was the paired fret adopted for small boxes because of lack of space in which to develop the running fret?

The difficulty of grouping pieces by common use of a single characteristic is that there are overlaps and contradictions. The distinctive floret edge that appears on two of the ripple group is found also on a four-lobed dish in Edinburgh, on another of the same shape that shows eight horses frolicking in a field, and on a square dish with deeply indented corners closely filled with a complicated and incoherent design of buildings and people (Lee, 1972: Pl. 120). Two others are shown in Krahl and Morgan (1989: Pls. 8, 10), but the floret edge is rare until it re-appears on some Qing pieces. If we assume the ripple group is fourteenth-century, can we place all the floret-edged pieces there? With the possible exception of the square dish, which is very odd (but

then odd examples crop up in all Chinese art forms), they could all be of about the same date.

But possibly we are wrong in trying to group idiosyncrasies on a time scale and should think of them as being characteristic of individual workshops. If we do that we can more easily accept the appearance of features apparently typical of distinct periods on the same piece. But although the names of several centres of lacquer production are known, we are a long way from knowing what was made where. One source of confusion could be over the conflicting claims of the Yangtze valley and Beijing to be the source of the 'official' wares. It is reasonable to suppose that the Yuan emperors, when their capital was at Beijing, were supplied to some extent by lacquer workshops set up in the neighbourhood, and it is inherently probable that not all the workers migrated to the south when the Ming set up their capital at Nanjing. The probability that Beijing remained a major lacquer-producing centre is increased by the fact that it was the princedom and base of Hongwu's son, who soon after his father's death was to usurp the throne as Yongle. There is therefore a likelihood that a distinct Yuan tradition from the north and a different Song tradition from the south ran parallel and mingled. When we add to this the fact that there were other lacquer workshops throughout the vast empire producing luxury goods, not for the emperor's court but for the scarcely less luxurious courts of his several sons in their dispersed princedoms, it is clear that there was room for hybrid types.

Some of these individual pieces make the mainstream official landscapes seem a little pedestrian. The highly competent results of a factory overseer's requirement for 'the same again only different' are reminiscent of those seventeenth-century Dutch cabinet pictures produced in great numbers for the bourgeoisie which, although technically assured, suffer from a certain sameness.

CHAPTER 10

DETAILS OF XUANDE STYLE

There is much to be said for Low Beer's view that because styles do not change with emperors we should make our attributions more general, 'first half of the fourteenth century' and so on; but though it may be illogical there is a case too for at least attempting a more narrow definition of styles. There are some characteristics of mid-fifteenth-century lacquer that it is convenient to call Xuande.

The great reputation of the ceramics of this reign tends to make one forget how short it was. For a mere nine years the twenty-one lacquer pieces attributed to it in the Beijing catalogue seem disproportionate. It is difficult to form a coherent view of a Xuande style from those twenty-one; some attributed to Xuande might just as well be Yongle and, indeed, the reverse is true for several Yongle pieces have a Xuande look about them.

Is there a distinctive Xuande style? The finest piece of undoubted Xuande lacquer, in Garner's view the finest piece of lacquer known, is the Imperial Table in the Victoria and Albert Museum (Pl. 44). This was originally supposed to be Wanli until a Xuande mark was found in an inconspicuous position, a circumstance in favour of its authenticity, but the error in date by more than a century and a half shows how difficult and uncertain dating can be.

Using the table as a touchstone we can distinguish Xuande characteristics unlike those we associate with Yongle. The decoration on the table top is not freely conceived as in Yuan and Yongle flower dishes, but is balanced and repetitive. A tendency towards symmetry can be made out as the Yuan gave way to the Ming which, if it were a steady progression as it almost certainly was not, could by the time of Xuande have given rise to the symmetrical splendours of this table. Despite Garner's praise, which is warranted perhaps by the great skill with which so elaborate a piece is carved, the loss of naturalness and the close patterning with small features create a busy, restless air that tires the eye without delighting it. We are no longer aware of peony, chrysanthemum and so on, but only of a rhythmic repetition of shapes. This restlessness results also from another feature characteristic of Xuande but not limited to it, that is the emphasis of edges. A ridge is used to outline rocks in the Ren Box and is the normal way of showing clouds in all carved lacquer. In flower pieces the upturned edge first appears as the natural shaping of petals in lotus blooms and then extends to chrysanthemums and other flowers, but in the Xuande table all pretence at naturalness is given up and the obtrusive outlining of individual features is automatic and purely decorative. But not all the table top is treated in this

Plate 44 **Red Table**
There is an inconspicuous Xuande mark in the centre of the inside
rear apron. The contrasting styles of what is probably a late Xuande
piece are illustrated by the edge of the table top and the strongly
outlined carving of the drawer faces. Xuande. Height 78.2 cm,
length 119.5 cm.
Victoria and Albert Museum

Plate 45 **Lotus Leaf Dish**
Dishes of this distinctive form are rare and seem to be limited to
this dynasty. The elaborate wave background is remarkable for this
date. Xuande. Length 24.7 cm, width 15.7 cm, depth 2.8 cm.
Palace Museum, Beijing

way — the corners between the inner frame and the foliate cartouche are carved with smooth-edged leaves, a
change of style that has the effect of steadying the design and suggests a period of transition.

The reign of Xuande was a stabilising one after the ag-
gressive expansion of the first two Ming emperors. The
Emperor himself was a man of peace, a poet and a
painter; there was an intellectual atmosphere about his
court. In place of the great flower-and-bird dishes of
the fourteenth century there are dragons, hydras and
magic mushrooms; Buddhist and Daoist symbols and
Sanskrit inscriptions become the decorative themes.

Symmetry, symbolism and the visual restlessness of defined edges are not the only peculiarities of lacquer attributed to Xuande; there is also a greater variety of
shape. Circular boxes are now often oval in elevation
unlike the flat-topped cylinders of Yuan/Yongle.
Circular dishes, which in the later years of Yongle devel-

oped lobed edges, are now sometimes shaped like lotus
leaves *(Pl. 45)*. Quality is always of the highest.

Landscapes with a claim to be Xuande are not common. A dish showing a 'Daoist fairyland' in Beijing is so
close-packed with pavilions, rocks, trees and clouds that
there is little space left for the usual background diapers and it is doubly unusual in having a border of figures *(Pl. 46)*. Another very fine dish with a Daoist subject, exhibited by Bluett & Sons in 1989 (Krahl and
Morgan, 1989: Pl. 11) shows an almost equal desire to
cram full the picture space. This dish, given to the fourteenth century, seems because of the ridged edges to
the floral decoration, both in the cavetto and beneath
it, to be Xuande. On the other hand, the Daoist box in
the City of Aberdeen Museum *(Pl. 34)*, though unusually designed in a frontal sense with many figures, is not
particularly crowded and the shape, a flattened cylinder
with the usual floral border, points to Yongle.

In the earliest landscapes, those we call Yuan, there was
some difficulty in separating the diapers for land, water
and air; the distinction was not sufficiently clear and
the attempt to mark it by a deeply engraved line was
not successful. Early Ming landscapes, called Yongle, re-

Plate 46 ***Mallow-shaped Dish: A Daoist Landscape***
Pieces with Daoist features are generally of a crowded and complicated design. Compartmentalised lobed borders seem to be characteristic of late Yongle and of Xuande; they do not occur on dishes
attributed to the Yuan dynasty. Xuande. Diameter 34.3 cm, depth
4.3 cm.
Palace Museum, Beijing

Plate 47 **Box-lid**
Beneath the glowing rose-red surface there is a thicker layer of brown lacquer, beneath that is another red layer in which the background diaper is carved. Midway to the left of the bold rouleau that frames the lid is an engraved Xuande mark that appears to be contemporary with the lacquer. The returns of the lid have been broken off but enough remains to show that the sides were carved with a floral pattern against a plain dull-yellow ground. The veins of the leaves are shown double wherever the central spine is raised but the lines have been made with narrow knife strokes and they fail to meet in a point. Open patterns with a diaper ground are sometimes found in Xuande pieces as in plate 35, but become more common towards the middle of the fifteenth century. Xuande. Length 65.5 cm, width 25 cm.
Private collection

lied upon the placing of a garden fence to mark the boundary between land and water, and made use of rocky headlands, trees and rooftops to keep water and air apart. But at some time, possibly in the third decade of the fifteenth century, the carvers hit upon the device of outlining the land with a narrow edge of red and carving the water beyond at a lower level. This technique was so successful that it has been widely used ever since. Pieces with a Xuande reign mark are of both types. Of the three-tiered boxes in Beijing attributed to Xuande, in the first, land and air are separated in the usual way though rather clumsily by a fence; in a second, land and sky are kept apart by trees and rocks, and the land is marked off from the water by a red line and a change in level; and in the third, air and water are only partially separated by a headland. The first is a typical gardenscape with sides of the ridged floral type; the other two are a departure from the official garden scene. In one a fisherman sits patiently under a full moon, and in the other a pleasure boat with sages shielded by an awning is being propelled across a lake. A tiered box in Aberdeen with a standard type of landscape has the red line separating land from water but the division between water and air is not marked *(Pl. 36)*. It is more finely finished than those at Beijing and has superior floral sides. Perhaps the whole group straddles the reigns and should be called Yongle/Xuande.

Nor are we on certain ground with the flower pieces. The magnificent dish in the Ashmolean Museum at Oxford has a Xuande mark carved in the base but would otherwise be thought to be late Yongle *(Pl. 25)*, whereas, in contrast, the box-lid *(Pl. 47)* which also has a Xuande mark has opened out in a broad confident sweep of two pheasants among peonies in the free and decorative way that became more common in the mid-fifteenth century. Both pieces can be supported by other examples and it is probable that both are Xuande, evidence of a period of transition.

The other departure that seems to have taken place in this reign is typical of the end of it because it is so rare. There is a cylindrical box in Beijing (Palace Museum, 1985: Pl. 99) with a fairly elaborate gardenscape and the usual ingredients in which the background diapers of both water and air are dark green. It is a well-designed piece in which the outline of the land, more strongly shaped than usual, is marked by a thin edging of red and the usual uncomfortable junction of water and air has been avoided by extending a headland across until it meets a tree. The border is the normal one of flowers against a yellow ground and were it not for the introduction of the green it would probably be called Yongle. If the box were alone, this attribution might be doubted but it is supported by a well-known box that has the Xuande reign mark carved in a rectangular cartouche on the face near the top edge *(Pl. 48)*. The naturalistic design of orioles in a crab-apple tree is distinguished by the way in which details of the leaves,

the fruit and the birds are picked out with black, green and a brighter tone of red. The same contrasting colours are used on the sides of lid and box but the variegated band of leaves and fruit is set as usual against a plain yellow ground. There is a superficial likeness here to the Japanese kamakura-bori in which the upper layer of lacquer is rubbed through to expose a contrasting tone beneath in order to simulate age.

During the Xuande period a number of Chinese lacquer workers went to Japan to study a polychrome technique that had been developed there. In the reign of Xuande's successor a member of a celebrated clan of lacquer workers in the lower Yangtze valley joined the workshop in Beijing and became known for his development of the imported technique. Japanese connoisseurs were said to prefer his work to that of their own masters. It may be that it was this contact with Japan that gave Chinese lacquer an impetus in a new direction. But what was it?

CHAPTER 11

HONGZHI AND THE PALACE LANDSCAPE

In the eighty-seven years between the end of Xuande's reign (1435) and the beginning of Jiajing's (1522) there are only two marked pieces, both Hongzhi (1488–1505). This means that the reign marks of Zhengtong (1436–49), Jingtai (1450–57), Tianshun — the title of the restored Zhengtong (1457–64) — and Chenghua (1465–87) are not seen on carved lacquer although a lacquer box inlaid with mother-of-pearl is dated to the last year of Chenghua. No one will suppose that carved lacquer was not made during those years, the marking of pieces, even those clearly designed for imperial use seems to have been quite arbitrary, perhaps at the whim of the factory overseer or even of individual artists.

Where so little positive evidence is available one looks where one can for pointers to what was happening. Xuande's son, Zhengtong, became emperor at the age of eight and a de facto regency was set up with the Empress Dowager, Xuande's mother, and Wang Zhen, Zhengtong's tutor, as dominant members. The fourteen years of their strong, conservative rule has been called the best-governed period of the whole dynasty and it would be reasonable to suppose that lacquer produced for the court during that time would have continued in the Xuande tradition. In fact, a few pieces in the style of the 'Oriole Box' *(Pl. 48)* which are loosely described as 'mid-Ming' would very happily fit here.

In 1448 an order was given that no porcelain should be made for private sale, presumably because the kilns had failed to satisfy the palace's orders since private trade was more profitable. If lacquer workers were subject to a similar restriction it would account for the almost complete absence of examples attributed to this period outside the Beijing hoard. Zhengtong, having assumed full powers, led a disastrous expedition against the Mongols beyond the northern frontier and was taken prisoner. Treated in a friendly fashion by his captors he was allowed to return to China to find that his half-brother had proclaimed himself emperor and did not welcome his return. For six years Zhengtong was held prisoner until he was released by a palace coup to reign, under the name of Tianshun, for a further eight years. Neither Zhengtong nor his usurping brother seem to have been interested in the arts. It may be that Tianshun had a speculative turn, for it was during his reign that Buddhist and Daoist classics were reprinted. However, there is no evidence that religious emblems were more commonly used at this time than under Xuande and it is unlikely that the character of either emperor influenced the design of lacquer.

Plate 48 **Polychrome Box: Two Orioles in a Crab Apple Tree**
Marked at 12 o'clock with a Xuande reign mark. Without the evidence of this marked box it would be difficult to establish that polychrome pieces were as early as Xuande. The conspicuous placing of the reign mark on the surface of the box is however typical of Xuande porcelain, although it cannot be paralleled in lacquer, and should be accepted as genuine. Xuande. Diameter 28.7 cm, depth 18.9 cm.
Palace Museum, Beijing

The interest of the middle and later years of the fifteenth century is not in the lacquer that continues or echoes the close patterns of the Xuande table, but in the naturalistic treatment of flowers and birds and in the development of a more fresh and open landscape. Both are likely to be features of the reign of Zhengtong's son, Chenghua.

The artistic climate of a court does not necessarily depend upon the character and taste of the monarch. Chenghua succeeded to the throne at the age of eighteen and was guided by a strong regency council. He was not a strong personality but his reign is one of the great cultural periods of the Ming. The temper of thought of the time was influenced by the philosopher-teacher, Chen Xianzhang. Chen was interested in painting and was himself a good calligrapher, but it was through his 'search after truth' that he commanded a following of important disciples who exercised an influence in the Palace that he never directly had. His philosophy, achieved after twenty years of solitary study, was based on the principle of 'being natural'. He owed a great deal to Song writers and to the ancient doctrine of quietism. He taught the 'one-ness' of man with nature. His rejection of traditional modes and his insistence that a man should search out his own path to the truth led to a minor artistic revolution not unlike that which took place under the Pharaoh Akhnaton.

Plate 49 **Square Tray: Natural Landscape**
Landscapes without the staffage of buildings or people are rare and
seem to be limited to the mid- to late fifteenth century. Chenghua.
25.9 cm.
Palace Museum, Beijing

As there are no pieces reign-marked Chenghua other than one piece of lacquer inlaid with mother-of-pearl, it is necessary to guess the progression from the formal designs of Xuande to the most extreme examples of naturalism, which I believe to be typical of the last three or four decades of the fifteenth century. Once more it is from Beijing that the best examples come. A densely designed square tray in which plants and trees, rooted in the ground and among rocks, grow out of the picture space at the top and fill it in a contrived way, has a free unrepetitive natural air (Palace Museum, 1985: Pl. 123). Even the two birds that perch inconspicuously among the branches are not pheasants, peacocks or phoenixes, but humble woodland birds of no very decorative kind. The dish in plate 49, if contrasted with that in plate 26, shows how great a change has taken place. The extreme development is seen in a set of trays that illustrate the four seasons (Pl. 50). Sprays of the appropriate flower enter the picture from outside the frame, the background is a four/six diaper and space is

Plate 50 **Red Tray: Spring**
One of a set of four trays at Beijing representing the seasons. The asymmetric naturalistic arrangement with the spray growing from beyond the picture space is the conception of a painter rather than a designer. Chenghua. 18.1 cm.
Palace Museum, Beijing

used in a way that is new in lacquer but reaches back to Song painting (Pl. 51). This straying of foliage in and out of the picture space occurs on a number of bowls and such minor pieces as the saucer in plate 52. They are the designs of a painter accustomed to work on silk or porcelain, not of a routine lacquer designer in a strictly controlled government factory. There are several examples of this free natural style in the Palace Museum, Beijing, but few of importance elsewhere (Pl. 53).

It is a short step from these trays to the charming landscape in plate 55 where neither man nor his works intrude. Of the same enchanting kind are two square

Plate 51 **Painting: Bird on Bough**
An album leaf painted in colours on silk. Song. Width 26, height 22 cm.
Eumorfopolous Collection, British Museum

landscape trays, alive with Chinese humour, which show boys managing their herds of water buffaloes (Palace Museum, 1985: Pls. 132, 133). These are something new, very different from the contemplative wine-bibbing scholars of Yuan and Yongle garden scenes.

Of a more common sort, one represented in many collections, is the small double-sided box that has no plain lacquered base but is carved over its whole surface, often with plum blossom or lychees on both sides but sometimes with landscapes. Occasionally these round boxes are straight-sided with distinct borders of flowers and leaves but more often they are rounded at the edge and a lychee decoration spreads over the top and down the sides to meet a similar design on the base. In its later development the box becomes an oval in eleva-

tion, a form that recurs in the nineteenth century. Very early circular boxes are flattened on top and slightly dished on the underside *(Pl. 56)* whereas the nineteenth-century versions which are carved top and bottom sit unsteadily on an uneven base.

Landscapes with the standard ingredients, which had become tedious by the reign of Xuande, enjoyed a revival after the mid-fifteenth century. It was as though lacquer designers, freed from traditional restraints, allowed their imaginations to play with the old forms. The modest pavilion grew into a palace, the lone sage

Plate 53 **Red Dish**
In naturalistic designs of this period the splendid stylised pheasants and legendary birds of the Yuan and early Ming are replaced by humble brown birds of the sparrow type or by modest water fowl. Chenghua. Diameter 12.6 cm.
Palace Museum, Beijing

Plate 52 a, b **Saucer**
This pretty piece belongs to the group in which the foliage decoration moves in and out of the frame-space. There is a thick black line between the foliage and the background. The interlocking petals that surround the central flower derive from the stylised lotus of the type seen on Southern Song porcelain and on the Yuan Juyong Gate north of Beijing, and are also on a pair of red lacquer stem cups carved with a motif of a playing child, which are marked Xuande. The carving of foliage is similar to that in plates 54 and 55. Late fifteenth-century. Diameter 11.5 cm.
Private collection

Plate 54 **The Dancing Asiatic**
'Watered silk' surface and black guideline are clearly visible. Other examples of this curious scene of a western Asiatic dancing and a lion are known (Wang, 1987: Pl. 57; Wirgin, 1972: Pl. 17; Krahl and Morgan, 1989: Pl. 25; and another with Moss). There are variations in all five. In the present box the scene is reversed and both box and lid are rimmed. The 'wrap-over' form of boxes is rare in the Palace Museum, Beijing, where the rimmed form is the rule. Late fifteenth-century or earlier. Diameter 8.3 cm, depth 3.7 cm.
Private collection

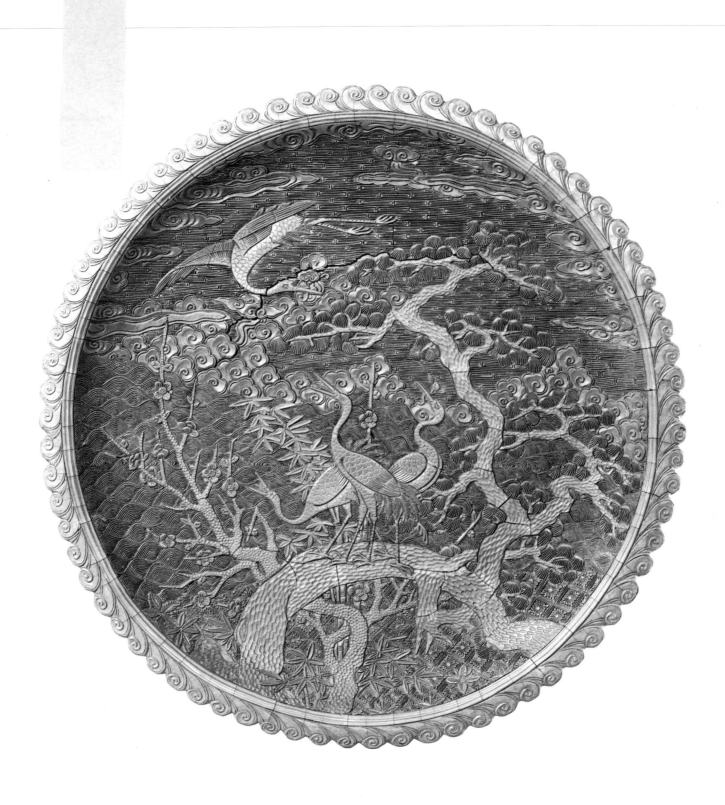

Plate 55 **Red Dish**
One of a set of three in Beijing showing pine, bamboo, plum blossoms and cranes (the symbol of high civil officials). This is the only one of the three to retain its unique flanged border. The carving is shallow but the design is more elegant and less tortured than much of the work of the reign. The other two dishes carry an elaborate inscription on the reverse. All three dishes are contemporary; the inscriptions were added later. Jiajing mark. Diameter 26.2 cm.
Palace Museum, Beijing

Plate 56 *Narcissus Box*

Red on yellow ground. There is an incised Yongle mark. It is a surprise to find so naturalistic a design of flowers as early as Yongle but there is a similar use of narcissi on a dish in Beijing (Palace Museum, 1985: Pl. 8), which is attributed there to late Yuan or early Ming, and a very similar bowl is called Yongle (*ibid*: Pl. 44). Yongle. Diameter 12.7 cm, depth 5 cm.
British Museum

Plate 57 *Box-lid*

Boxes of this type are thought to have been used to contain marriage documents. A box in the Victoria and Albert Museum (Strange, 1925: Pl. 20) with some similar characteristics represents episodes in a betrothal. It has been suggested by Craig Clunas that the present landscape represents the arrival of the bridegroom at a palace where the bride's parents await him; but it might equally well be held to celebrate the return of a son from a successful journey. The colour is particularly deep and rich and a very wide range of diapers has been used. This box-lid is similar in certain respects to that in the collection of the Cleveland Museum of Art, 'Purification at the Orchid Pavilion'. Zhengtong/Tianshun. Length 65.5 cm, width 24 cm.
Private collection

Plate 58 Dish: The Orchid Pavilion of Prince Tang
Red on a yellow ground. Dated over doorway to 1489 and inscribed
on vertical posts 'Made by Wang Ming' and 'Pingliang' (a town in
Gansu which is thought to have been the artist's birthplace).
Carved on the base in black lacquer within a square frame is a long
inscription describing Prince Tang's Orchid Pavilion. In the seg-
ments beyond the frame are patterns of magic mushrooms. The reverse of the cavetto is divided into four decorative cartouches containing landscapes and figures. The cartouches are separated by
three-clawed dragons alternating with phoenixes. Hongzhi.
Diameter 18.8 cm.
British Museum

Plate 59 **Polychrome box**
Black over red on a yellow ground. Inscribed with the name of the
same artist, Wang Ming, and village as 'The Orchid Pavilion of
Prince Tang' *(Pl. 58)*. Hongzhi. Diameter 31.8 cm.
Freer Gallery of Art

Plate 60 **Polychrome Box**
Red over dark green and yellow. Low Beer (1952) pointed out that this has so much in common with the dated dish in plate 58 that it is clearly a product of the same workshop at approximately the same time. Other pieces that relate both to 'The Orchid Pavilion of Prince Tang' dish and to this box are in the Freer Gallery of Art *(Pl. 59)*, in Tokyo (Tokyo National Museum, 1977), Los Angeles County Museum (Kuwayama, 1982), and in Beijing (Palace Museum, 1985). With plates 61 and 65, they form a group attributable to the atelier of Wang Ming at Pingliang. Hongzhi. Diameter 22.4 cm, depth 10.5 cm.
Linden-Museum, Stuttgart

seated at a table became an emperor with his consort, the visiting friends became a train of high dignitaries mounted on horses and the scene was set against a credible distance *(Pl. 57)*.

The key to the dating of these pieces is a famous dish in the British Museum, 'The Orchid Pavilion of Prince Tang', which is dated over a doorway to the second year of Hongzhi, 1489 *(Pl. 58)*. On the base there is a poem in black relief identifying the pavilion. The carver names himself on the front of the dish as Wang Ming, and beside his signature is the name of a village in Gansu, the central-western province that is presumed to have been his birthplace. An undated piece without a reign mark but inscribed with the name of the same

artist and the same village is in the Freer Gallery of Art, Washington, DC *(Pl. 59)*. It is reasonable to suppose that both were made in Gansu. Garner attributed two others to this workshop — a box in Stuttgart *(Pl. 60)* and another in the British Museum *(Pl. 61)*. There are others that seem to be related. A desk screen in the Tokyo National Museum is signed Wang Yan who, it is suggested, was the brother of Wang Ming. There is a very similar screen in Los Angeles (Kuwayama, 1982: Pl. 20). The 'Battle Stem Cup' *(Pl. 65)* is certainly from this factory.

These pieces, the list is not exhaustive, do not have all characteristics in common but they are sufficiently closely connected in one way or another with 'The Orchid Pavilion of Prince Tang' to suggest a relationship. Two features are common to them all. The first is an obvious attempt at naturalism — the use of an extraordinary wave diaper in which the undulating form has become exaggerated into a hump, instead of the formal geometric symbol. These diapers are not alike, some are more freely drawn than others, but in each case the distortion is apparent. The second common feature is the exuberant nature of the buildings. They are of two types. The dated piece, the box in Stuttgart, and the one in the Freer Gallery, have the exaggeratedly upswept eaves that are a distinctive feature of the

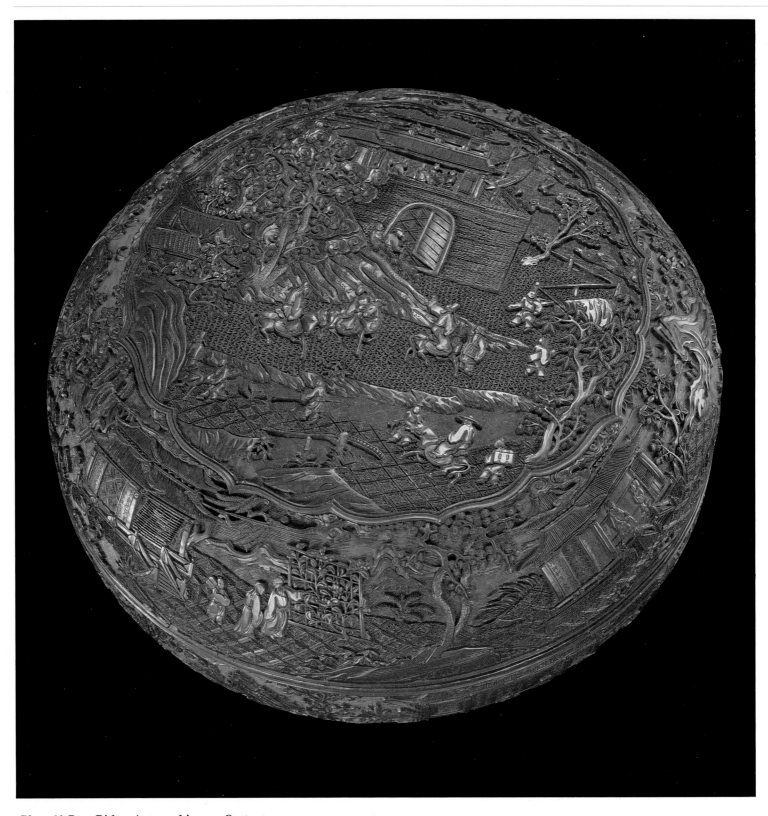

Plate 61 **Box: Riders Approaching an Outpost**
Carved in the same miniaturist style as plate 58. The under-edge of
the box is decorated with a continuous landscape. Hongzhi.
Diameter 27.4 cm.
British Museum

Plate 62 **Red Dish: Elaborate Palace**
Although dissimilar in some respects, the exaggerated wave diaper
and the extraordinary elaboration of the palace relate this piece to
the Pingliang group. Hongzhi mark. Diameter 17.7 cm.
Palace Museum, Beijing

Plate 63 **Red Oblong Box:
The Yue Yang Tower**
By far the finest of the pieces attributable to
the Wang atelier at Pingliang. The extensive
landscape with buildings is continued along
the sides of both box and lid. Hongzhi.
Length 60 cm, width 25 cm, depth 21 cm.
Palace Museum, Beijing

Plate 64 **Red Box: The Teng Wang Pavilion**
The representation of elaborate mythical or
historic buildings became fashionable towards the end of the fifteenth century. Some
examples are rather crowded and are carved
in what is almost a miniature style; others
such as this example are magnificently
carved in the same bold manner as plate 63.
Hongzhi. Length 43 cm, width 28.3 cm,
depth 9.5 cm.
Palace Museum, Beijing

architecture of south China, while the British Museum box has the more modest eaves typical of the north.

With this group we seem to be in the presence of a distinctive artistic personality. It is not necessary that Wang Ming and Wang Yan should have been directly responsible for all pieces of the type, others about them will have worked in a similar style.

The pieces associated with the Wangs have an individuality that marks them out as the product of a provincial atelier, but a somewhat similar development had taken place in the 'official' wares. The only other piece with a Hongzhi reign mark is in Beijing *(Pl. 62)*. It shows a strangely extravagant palace on the shore of a sea where a storm-tossed boat rides hump-backed waves. Although the building is not named it clearly has individual significance. The standardisation imposed by the government factory led to unsurpassed technical excellence but did not allow of landscape portraiture. But by the second half of the fifteenth century we are no longer shown any garden pavilion but 'The Orchid Pavilion of Prince Tang', an imaginative reconstruction no doubt, but still a form of portraiture. A splendid oblong rectangular box in Beijing *(Pl. 63)* portrays 'The Yue Yang Tower' and a related stationery box 'The Teng Wang Pavilion' *(Pl. 64)*. 'The Orchid Pavilion' recurs in a box-lid at Cleveland Museum of Art. Other buildings, unnamed, were probably recognisable to the informed connoisseur.

The two named boxes in Beijing are surely official pieces in as much as the standard of craftsmanship is very high but they differ significantly in the carving of the rocks. 'The Teng Wang Pavilion' stands among rocks only slightly dished at the edges, a characteristic of all the finest of the pieces attributable to Chenghua, whereas those of 'The Yue Yang Tower' have a raised relief outline. The box-lid in plate 57, superbly carved in an unusually rich dark crimson colour, has a strong stylistic affinity to 'The Teng Wang Pavilion' and shares with it a liveliness in the figures despite the bold simplicity with which they are carved.

The landscapes of these three pieces are more extensive, airy and individually conceived than the official gardenscapes of Yongle. That the type is less well known is in part because they are so rare outside the Beijing Palace collection. In many ways the most varied, skilful and interesting lacquer was made not in the time of Yongle and Xuande but in the second half of the fifteenth century, in the reigns of Chenghua and Hongzhi.

Plate 65 a, b **The Battle Stem Cup**
Red lacquer over a layer of black above a yellow base. The miniature pictorial style, the freely drawn unconventional diapers, the elaboration of the theme, the strong diagonal, and the linear detailing of the rocks all point directly to the Wang Ming atelier at Pingliang. Hongzhi. Diameter 15 cm, height 10.5 cm.
Private collection

CHAPTER 12

MARKED PIECES OF THE MID AND LATE MING

At some point there seems to be a sharp transition from typical fifteenth-century wares to those that are known to be sixteenth-century.

There are no marked pieces of the reign of Zhengde (1506–21), who seems to have had no aesthetic interests. There is no direct evidence of carved lacquer made in the fifteen years of his reign, which is a no-man's-land between the palatial landscapes of Hongzhi and the restless symbols of Jiajing. There is however a small group that does not accord with what we know of either Hongzhi or of Jiajing. The small tray in plate 66, 'The Necromancer', is carved in two shades of red lacquer on a solid wooden base. The unusual lobed shape has a near equivalent in Beijing (Palace Museum, 1985: Pl. 256) which also has a solid rounded gallery, but whereas that gallery is edged with Buddhist emblems 'The Necromancer' has a roughly carved key-fret. The Palace Museum calls its tray 'late-Ming'. Another distinctive feature of 'The Necromancer' tray is the carving of the pine-clusters, normally the radial lines are straight but here they curve in a clockwise sense. There is one piece in Beijing that has this peculiarity, a brushpot carved with a 'Meeting of King Wen Wang and Jiang Shang by the Wei River' (*ibid*: Pl. 137), which is listed as 'mid-Ming'. Another brushpot in the Victoria and Albert Museum in which the radial lines curve in

the same way is called 'early seventeenth-century'. In Taibei, there is a small round box with figures of the Seven Sages riding in a landscape with the same curved pine-needles (National Palace Museum, 1981: Pl. 15). This is marked Xuande, which is improbable, although interestingly it is a very crowded design as in the Xuande Daoist pieces already mentioned.

Lee Yu-kuan illustrated two examples (1979: Pls. 125, 184) of which I do not know the present whereabouts. One, an oblong cosmetic box in three sections, a broadly carved piece in which the top and sides are decorated with varying motifs, landscapes, formalised dragons and plum blossoms, he called Chenghua. Not only are the pine-cones of the curved type, but the very bold carving of rocks and figures is like that in the tray. The other, a red rectangular incense box with landscape top and floral sides, Lee Yu-kuan called Japanese of the Momoyama or early Edo period, an attribution that I do not think would be generally accepted. The carving of pine-cluster and rock are much the same as in the oblong cosmetic box and 'The Necromancer' tray, but the only diaper used is the four/six air diaper, which stands here indiscriminately for air and water. The use of diapers as a decorative background without reference to their representational significance is, generally, a feature of sixteenth-century lacquer.

Plate 66 **Small Tray: The Necromancer**
Bright full red over a ground of deep red on a solid wooden base.
The figures, deep, broad and stylised, are exaggeratedly slit-eyed
and have extraordinarily long ear lobes. This last feature is paralleled in an oval dish, 'The Washing of the White Elephant', in the
Castle Kemp Foundation, Ekalsund, Sweden, which bears a Jiajing
mark (Wirgin, 1972). Zhengde/Jiajing? Maximum width 17.4 cm,
vertical breadth 16 cm, depth 2.5 cm.
Private collection

Plate 67 **Red Oblong Tray: Man Gathering Medicinal Herbs**
By the middle of the fifteenth century landscapes no longer show philosophers admiring waterfalls, instead there are more elaborate and varied scenes of husbandry or play or historic occasions. Zhengtong/Jingtai. Length 35.4 cm, width 15.4 cm, depth 2.7 cm.
Palace Museum, Beijing

Plate 68 **Bowl**
Dated to 1541 by an incised inscription on the base which also tells us that the bowl was made for 'the use of the Tao family'. It is late for this form of coupled key-fret to appear on a bowl of this size. Jiajing. Diameter 25.3 cm, height 9.5 cm.
Helen Foresman Spencer Museum of Art, University of Kansas

Plate 69 **Leys Jar**
This elaborate and distinctive piece bears on the base, incised in large gilt letters, the signature of Wu Baosu. No other signed lacquer by this artist is known but an ink-maker of that name is recorded and since ink-makers are known also to have carved lacquer this is presumably the same man. According to Paul Moss (Moss, 1986) 'the bulbous lower section, foot and back are lacquered on a metal base, while the rim is built up from a lighter construction which must have had a wood base, perhaps with cloth.' A similar but unsigned jar in Beijing is called 'mid-Qing' (Palace Museum: Pl. 294). The style is consistent with earlier Jiajing, but an inkstone dated 1628 is know and if this Wu Baosu is the same man, an early Jiajing date is unlikely and that of the last Ming emperor, Chongzhen, becomes possible. The fine carving argues for the earlier date. Jiajing. Height 14.5 cm, diameter 17.2 cm.
Sidney L. Moss Ltd.

Yet another peculiarity of 'The Necromancer' tray is the carving of the hands. In nearly all fifteenth- and sixteenth-century figures the hands are concealed, or shown as inconspicuously as possible, but the hands of the necromancer and of the servant before him are an expressive feature of the design. There is a similar carving of hands in Beijing's tray, 'A Man Gathering Medicinal Herbs' *(Pl. 67)* and the figures on a small round box in Budapest seem to be by the same hand (Budapest Museum of Applied Arts, 1981: No. 93). The Beijing tray is called there 'mid-Ming'. In this tray two levels of flower diaper are used to represent earth, water and air, exactly as in 'The Necromancer' tray, and the tree-trunk is carved in the same scaly manner, but the pine-needles are straight.

These small clues may seem to amount to very little but if not relied upon too heavily they serve to identify lacquer of the first quarter of the sixteenth century. Pieces loosely called 'mid-Ming' should be studied for parallels — after all, there is nothing much more mid-Ming than Zhengde.

Although there are no marks of Zhengde, those of Jiajing are common. I have a note of over fifty, but dated examples are rare. The earliest is a distinguished bowl in the Helen Foresman Spencer Museum of the

Plate 71 **Bowl**
The inside and base are in brownish-black lacquer. There is a Wanli mark in the centre of the base. It is closely related to plate 68, the dated piece of Jiajing. Wanli. Diameter 11.6, height 6 cm.
Museum of Far Eastern Antiquities, Stockholm

Plate 70 a, b **The Barbarian Dish**
This is remarkable in many ways. The centre is recessed inside a raised boss and is decorated against a bright gold (not yellow) ground with the kneeling figure of a barbarian bearing on his head what appears to be a tray and a ritual vessel. The underside of the dish is belled. The rim of running beasts and *lingzhi* fungus can be paralleled in Han metalwork, and the raised boss is reminiscent of Tang mirrors. The elaborate ribbon decoration and the relief carving are, as Low Beer noted, surely of the sixteenth century. All the carving is of superlative quality. Is this the work of the famous lacquerer, Huang Cheng of the mid-sixteenth century? Is it in any way related to the 'Dancing Asiatic' group *(Pl. 54)*? It is at least evidence of the influence of metalwork on lacquer design. Sixteenth-century. Diameter 17.5 cm, height 1.8 cm.
Linden-Museum, Stuttgart

University of Kansas, which is dated 1541, well into the reign *(Pl. 68)*. It has a flared lip and elegant cartouches separated by land diapers and is of fine quality. Within the cartouches are landscapes with birds, the tree-trunks are represented with scales as in 'The Necromancer' dish but the diapers are used in a representational sense. In one landscape cranes appear, birds that feature very often in Jiajing lacquers. In the Tang period cranes were known as ostriches and were symbols of the Vermilion Bird of the South, a creature associated with the sun and the colour red and also, possibly, a symbol of the empress. There is no reason to suppose that the crane (or ostrich) had any such significance nearly a thousand years later. The Chinese appetite for archaisms was immense even when their significance was not understood.

Other flared-lip bowls with cartouche decorations are in Stuttgart (Brandt, Pl. 54) and in Sweden *(Pl. 71)*. The Swedish bowl, which has a Wanli mark, is less elegant, less finely carved, more bulky in shape, but its scenes are jovial and delightfully light-hearted, breathing a very Chinese *joie de vivre*.

Jiajing wares have certain well-marked characteristics. They are often polychrome; reds tend to be dark and verge on brown. The colour change may be the result not so much of a change of taste as of a change in the source of supply of the lacquerer's raw material, which may also be responsible for the tendency of some Jiajing pieces to crack and flake. Floral borders, which in preceding reigns strayed beyond their boundaries,

Plate 72 **Ring-shaped Box**
A rare shape made perhaps to contain a headband or a bracelet.
The carving is deep and vertical. The typical tripartite rocks are re-
peated four times on the inward face of both rings. Jiajing. Outer
diameter 16.4 cm, inner diameter 5.7 cm, depth 7 cm.
Private collection

are now designed with a continuous tendril, a wreath
confined within borders. Shapes are often eccentric
and show how restless was the search for novelty
(Pl. 72). Deep boxes are strongly lobed and tiered; rims
are usually grooved; so-called rice-measures, sometimes
six- or eight-sided, widening towards the top, look like
collapsible waste-paper baskets. The carving of early
pieces if of the highest quality but later it becomes
steeper and more peremptory, sharper edged, and is
usually without the smooth polish of the previous
century.

The quality varies a good deal — the box in plate 72 is
solid and well-finished — but some of the better pieces,
such as the Kansas bowl, show cracks. The most con-

spicuous feature of the later part of the reign is the limited subject-matter. Jiajing, a man of literary tastes
rather than a painter, began his reign by expelling
Buddhism from the Forbidden City and installing
Daoism in its place, and it is owing to the influence of
Daoist magic that the favourite motifs of the reign are
characters signifying long life, happiness and good
luck. Long life, the ultimate good of most Chinese, particularly concerned Jiajing — a dangerous passion for
he died from the use of a drug that he believed to be
the elixir of immortality, possibly one that contained
liquid lacquer.

Another feature of later Jiajing lacquer that persists well
into the reign of Wanli is the tripartite vertical rock,
often curled about with waves, which whenever possible
is introduced at six o'clock of the design like a brand
mark. This may originally have represented Mount
Sumeru, sacred to Buddhism, or the Foundations of
the World, or the Islands of the Blest, but had probably
deteriorated into a superstitious symbol like crossed fin-

Plate 73 *Splat of Folding Chair*
Red lacquer. The forward-facing dragon and the tripartite rocks
with breaking waves urge a Jiajing date; the footstool belonging to
this chair, however, is convincingly Xuande (Garner, 1979: Pl. 82).
The Xuande reign mark seems to have been cut when the chair
was made. It may be that the chair was a later replacement of a
Xuande chair related to the table in plate 44 and the footstool,
being undamaged, survived. It would have seemed natural to re-
peat the original mark on the replacement while at the same time
bringing the detail of the decoration up to date. Jiajing? Height
27 cm, width 16.5 cm.
Victoria and Albert Museum

*Plate 74 **Box: Well-wishing Gods at a Birthday Party***
Red lacquer against a ginger-coloured diapered ground . A delightful scene of celestial jollification. The tortured shapes of the trees
are typical of the mid-sixteenth century. Jiajing mark. Diameter
39.5 cm, depth 10 cm.
Palace Museum, Beijing

*Plate 75 **Deep Dish***
Within the red recessed foot there is a gilt reign mark of Longqing.
Marks of this reign are very rare. The small forward-facing dragon's
head just beyond the jaws of the imperial five-clawed dragon is
unique, its significance unknown. The meandering floral border
typical of Wanli was evidently introduced in this reign. A cup-stand
of related style is in the Maidstone Museum. Longqing. Diameter
38.5, height 7.5 cm.
British Museum

gers and may have derived as an admired decorative
feature from the Xuande folding chair in plate 73.
Landscapes are rare, a few show extravagantly bizarre
buildings of a Daoist fairyland while others are country
scenes of bucolic humour. Three dishes in Beijing
showing cranes amongst trees have a freshness and an
engaging sense of fun *(Pl. 55)*, while 'Five Old Men
Enjoying a Birthday Party' (Palace Museum, 1985:
Pl. 219) and 'Well-wishing Gods at a Birthday Party'
(Pl. 74) are hilarious. They are probably early. Nor are
there any of the dense flower-and-bird dishes of 100
years before, instead five-clawed dragons, symbols of
the emperor, and phoenixes, symbols of the empress
(of whom there were successively four), appear in great
abundance and often in association. Jiajing dragons are
narrow, rather mean and snake-like, contorted but not
strong, often full-faced or with a snout that ends
strangely in a vertical growth. Designs are no longer co-
ordinated to give one grand visual impression but are
simply ways to fill the available space with emblems and
symbols that require 'reading'. On the whole lacquer of
the Jiajing period is restless; it catered for a jaded palate
with a taste for mannerism. Characteristic of the period
is the ridged rim which is rarely seen on the lacquer of
Wanli.

There are few pieces of carved lacquer with the reign
mark of Longqing (1567–72). One, a deep dish in the
British Museum *(Pl. 75)*, is peculiar in that the bodiless
head of a small be-whiskered dragon appears about to
be swallowed by a five-clawed imperial dragon. The reference, no doubt clear in the Palace at the time, has es-
caped later enquirers. Otherwise this dish has the vertical rocks surrounded by breaking waves common to
late Jiajing and to Wanli, and a long tendrilled flower
border that does not seek to escape its frame. It is of
good quality but is otherwise not remarkable. Another,
a plum-blossom-shaped polychrome box with cloud and
dragon motifs is in the National Palace Museum,

Taiwan *(Pl. 76)*. Yet another dish is in the Lee Family Collection (Lee King Tsi: Pl. 61).

There is a reference in Gao Lian's *Eight Discourses on the Art of Living* to a noted lacquerer of this reign, Huang Cheng *(fl. 1567–72)*, the author of a technical treatise on lacquering, whose work was already 'being copied by lesser men'. This suggests that his designs were distinctive but they have not yet been identified, unless that in plate 70 is an example.

The reign of Wanli (1573–1619), covering forty-six years, gave ample scope for changes of subject and style. The trouble is that we do not certainly know what they are, for although more dated pieces have survived from this reign than from any other there are none

from the earliest years and only one from the later. The first, dated 1586, is a bowl in Stuttgart *(Pl. 77)*. It is less elegantly shaped and finished than the Jiajing bowl of 1541 but otherwise very similar, which leads one to suppose that late Jiajing, Longqing and much Wanli lacquer may often be indistinguishable. On the other hand, a dish in the same museum dated to 1587 is unusual because its subject is a still life of fruit and flowers in what is clearly a lacquer bowl on a lacquer stand *(Pl. 78)*. The contrast between the very fine polychrome box in Los Angeles (Kuwayama, 1982: Pl. 27) and the box of the same date in Stuttgart shows the variety of quality and style that may be expected. But landscapes, certainly those as good as the Los Angeles box, are rare. Another landscape, perhaps from the same hand (there

is a similarity in the figure drawing), is the 'Seven Sages in the Bamboo Garden' tray in the Ashmolean Museum, Oxford *(Pl. 79)*.

The last dated piece of Wanli carved lacquer is 1619 (National Palace Museum, 1971: Pl. 14). Its diaper field is in fine detail but otherwise it differs little from pieces twenty-four years earlier.

Beyond the nominal and brief reign of Taichang (1620) of which, not surprisingly, nothing of lacquer interest is known, we descend into the valley of the Ming. Tianqi (1621–27) was an illiterate who was fond of

*Plate 76 a, b **Lobed Polychrome Box***
There is a Longqing mark on the cracked base. A third marked piece is shown in Lee King Tsi, Pl. 61 and a fourth was sold at Christie's in 1983 (Lot 59). No diaper is used for the background. Longqing. Diameter 22.5 cm.
National Palace Museum, Taibei

working with axe and saw, and 'with a knife to carve lacquer ware'. Whether he was any good at it is not recorded.

In the four volume novel *Golden Lotus*, thought to have been written in the reign of Tianqi, a secondary subject

is the interchange of gifts which are often described in some detail. Gold, silver, jade and bolts of cloth, especially silk, are the common coinage of bribery and gratitude, but never lacquer. There is also a revealing reference to a proverb: 'Forgery is not one of the recognised fine arts, yet there is no genuine lacquer to be found anywhere.' If the leys jar in plate 69 is from this reign — as it conceivably may be since Wu Baosu its putative carver also made an inkstick which is dated 1628 — then some excellent work was done. However, it must be admitted that the Jar sits very happily in the mid-sixteenth century and it may be that the ink-carver was a different man. Meanwhile, Tianqi, a pleasant but ineffectual man, was succeeded by his brother Chongzhen (1628–44) when the Manchus were already within the borders of the empire and rebellion was rife. When Beijing eventually fell to the invaders Chongzhen hanged himself on Coal Hill in the palace grounds and the Ming dynasty was ended.

Plate 77 **Bowl**
Red lacquer. There is a Wanli mark and the date of 1586. The squat heavy shape of this and most Jiajing and Wanli bowls contrasts with the shapeliness of plate 68. Wanli. Diameter 13.3 cm, depth 7 cm.
Linden-Museum, Stuttgart

Plate 78 **Still Life Dish**
There is a Wanli mark and the date of 1587. The subject is the most unusual one of fruit and flowers in a bowl-on-stand, not unlike that in plate 15. Wanli. An identical subject in porcelain is shown in Jenyns' *Ming Pottery and Porcelain*, Pl. 108. Diameter 25.8 cm, depth 4.4 cm.
Linden-Museum, Stuttgart

Plate 79 **Red Tray: Sages in a Bamboo Grove**
Upper red layer carved through to a plain yellow ground. Scroll
pattern in corners. The style of the figures is somewhat like those
on a Wanli box dated 1595 in Los Angeles (Kuwayama, 1982:
Pl. 27). The scene may depict a famous birthday party that was cele-
brated in Zhu Jing's garden in Beijing on 12 June 1499. Wanli.
Length 48 cm.
Ashmolean Museum, Oxford

Plate 80 **Polychrome Box**
There is a Wanli mark and the date of 1595. Several nearly identi-
cal boxes exist. One, of the same dimensions with the same date, is
in the City Museum and Art Gallery, Hong Kong (Garner, 1979).
Another, 31.2 cm in diameter and undated, is in the Freer Gallery
of Art. Five carved lacquer pieces of Wanli bear this same date
(Riddell, 1979). Wanli. Diameter 20.3 cm.
Robert Peters

Plate 81 **Red Dish: Gods and Demons in Battle**
This representation of demons seems to be unique in lacquer but
demonic creatures of a similar type are known in other media. Are
Chinese demons the source of the imaginings of Hieronymus
Bosch? The very simplified dragons around the border are charac-
teristic of Wanli. Wanli. Diameter 15.9 cm.
Palace Museum, Beijing

Plate 82 **Cloud-diaper Box**
Three other examples with this distinctive cloud-diaper are known,
all in the Lee Family Collection (Lee King Tsi, 1990: Pls. 67, 70,
71). The last of these is marked with a date corresponding to 1543.
The crowded composition and peremptory carving suggest an outland workshop. Are these sixteenth-century attempts at copying the
earlier wares of Yunnan? The second edition of the *Ge Gu Yao Lun*
(1462) asserts that there were already many imitations. If the mark
date of the Lee piece is authentic this must be Jiajing. Diameter
36.5 cm, depth 24 cm.
Bluett and Sons Ltd.

CHAPTER 13

YUNNAN WARE

The province of Yunnan in the extreme south-west of China was only periodically and uncertainly part of the empire. It is a highland country, rich in minerals but with limited agricultural wealth. *Rhus verniciflua* grows there as it does throughout China with the exception of the extreme north. The Yunnanese people are not Han, the majority race in China, but are of several ethnic minorities. The Yuan dynasty re-established authority over Yunnan and when their power in the rest of China disintegrated an independent Mongol state persisted there until it was subdued by Hongwu, the first of the Ming emperors.

There is a literary tradition that the Tang emperors sent lacquer workers from Sichuan, where there were two lacquer workshops under the Han, to establish the industry in this unlikely place. The long-established independent kingdom of Dali in the west of the province occasionally raided its great neighbour and it is more probable that when the people of Yunnan invaded Sichuan during the Tang period they took back as booty a number of lacquer workers. That lacquer-making was established in Yunnan at an early date is proved by the fact that among the tribute paid to the Song emperor by the Dali kingdom in 1076 was an article of carved lacquer. In the second edition of the *Ge Gu Yao Lun* (1462), the then prefect of Hangzhou, itself a centre of lacquer production, wrote: 'At the present day craftsmen of Dalifu in Yunnan are skilled in making this lacquer, but their products are copied elsewhere. Their work is often found in noble houses in Nanjing. There are two kinds, vermilion and darker red. Fine specimens are worth a lot, but one must watch out for imitations.'

The 'kind of lacquer' referred to was 'piled red' or bastard lacquer, a composition of lacquer and brick-dust. Shen Defu, scholar and connoisseur, wrote in 1606 of the lacquer made in the Guo Yuan factory at Beijing that there was another kind — dull, dark and poorly carved, known as Old Yunnan Lacquer — which in his opinion ought to be valued more highly than the wares from the palace factory in the north.

Despite the absence of evidence in modern Yunnan that a lacquer industry ever existed there, the evidence that it once did is overwhelming. It is less certain that the lacquer it made has been correctly identified. As to Old Yunnan, there is a reasonable chance that those pieces related to the Engakuji examples (*Pls. 12, 14*) are genuine Old Yunnan. The naïvety of their design is explicable if we accept that although lacquer workers were captured in Sichuan and taken to Yunnan the raiders neglected to take Tang designers with them.

It would be understandable if early fourteenth-century wares were no longer remembered in their home province, but less so that the large group of lacquers, now confidently termed Yunnan and supposed to be of the sixteenth and seventeenth centuries, had left no trace there. Yet, that lacquer was still being made in Yunnan in the sixteenth century we have the testimony of Shen Defu.

Fritz Low Beer, an acute observer, was the first to distinguish the group. He noted that they were all carved over smooth backgrounds:

'The design is always crowded and very little background is visible. Drawing and carving combine to give an impression of movement which might almost be called tortuous. The carver seems afraid of leaving any flat or smooth surfaces. Wherever the nature of the subject-matter permits he has cut

sharply inwards from the outlines, which are left as narrow ridges. The effect is increased through the use of many small details; larger ones are frequently broken up into many rows of ridges which are separated by deep cuts.'

It was Garner who first suggested that the group may have been made in Yunnan and then went on to assume that it was (Garner, 1979). But the references he used seem to have little relevance. It is probable that such pieces were made in Yunnan, but until some positive evidence is brought forward all that can be said with certainty is that they are the product of a distinctive factory that was technically proficient in an individual way, and that it was productive and commercially organised.

The Beijing catalogue illustrates ten pieces with Yunnan characteristics. All have the typical complicated and tor-

Plate 83 **Insect Box**
Red upon an ochre ground, black interior and base. The box is carved with a praying mantis and other insects, a lizard and a toad. There are six examples of this design recorded, its origin and significance is unknown. Garner proposed that the group was made in Yunnan. Early sixteenth-century? Diameter 38.8 cm, depth 8.8 cm.
Fitzwilliam Museum, Cambridge

Plate 84 **Eared Red Pot**
The crowded sharp carving is of the type generally called Yunnan. Although called mid-Ming in Beijing, the shape of this pot suggests the end of the seventeenth century. Possibly Kangxi. Length 36.2 cm, width 20.5 cm.
Palace Museum, Beijing

Plate 85 **The Small Insect Box**
From the same workshop as plates 86 and 87. It is, however, not carved all over but stands on a plain foot rim. The foundation is a combination of wood and composition. The lid is carved with eight insects of various kinds hidden among fruit and foliage. The dominant figure is a large cricket place centrally on the lid. From Sichuan. Late Ming. Diameter 12 cm, height 7.5 cm.
Private collection

Plate 86 **The Double-sided Squirrel Box**
The foundation is wood rimmed with brass. Colour and style of carving connect with the Small Insect Box *(Pl. 85)*, The Chess Players *(Pl. 87)* and a fourth box in the Národní Museum in Prague. Together they form the 'Sichuan Group' which, although related to the Yunnan Insect Group, is distinct from it. In all four boxes there is undercutting, a known feature of Yunnan work. Box and lid together have eight squirrels active among vines. Squirrels plundering grape vines is a favourite subject in many media. Lee Yu-kuan (1972) illustrates one in appliquéd lacquer from the Ryukyu Islands which he dates between 1715 and 1750. Possibly late seventeenth century. Diameter 12.5 cm, depth 6.2 cm.
Private collection

tured semi-barbaric design that at first glance is difficult to disentangle. We can reasonably assume that these ten pieces were made for the court. Did Yunnan lacquerers receive orders from Beijing? It seems improbable. Garner, in an article the purpose of which was to demonstrate that lacquer-masters worked from a common design, showed a box in the Freer Gallery *(Pl. 33)* and opposed to it a dish from the Low Beer collection (Garner, 1973a). Many features — pavilion, trees and figures — are the same, but although he noted that the carver of the Low Beer dish made some alterations he did not point out the great difference in the way the rocks are represented. An extraordinary convention for expressing rocks by a series of parallel close contours is typical of Yunnan. This appears on the Low Beer tray but not on the Freer box. Garner called both pieces early fifteenth-century, but the dish is surely later and inferior to the box. The tree is stiff and clumsy and the figures do not take a natural place in the landscape, re-

minding one of a painting in which one artist has done the background and another put in the figures. If, as is possible, the Low Beer tray is as late as the seventeenth century it may simply be that some Yunnan mannerisms had passed into the general vocabulary of the lacquer-makers and that the copyist of the time confused two traditional styles. The most likely explanation of the presence of Yunnan lacquers in the Beijing collection is that carvers from the Yunnan factory (if it were in Yunnan) had been transferred to whatever centre it was that made the 'official' wares. Is the tradition that craftsmen from Yunnan were sent to the government factory even as late as the Qing dynasty well-founded? The tall flattened vase with an eared neck in plate 84 has a mid-nineteenth-century look about it.

The Yunnan lacquerers repeated distinct motifs. A well-known tray in the Seattle Art Museum (Garner, 1979: Pl. 73) has a bamboo-like treatment of the rim which Garner called 'unusual'. An almost identical tray was il-

*Plate 87 a, b **The Chess Players***
The sides of the lid and box are decorated with a wreath of foliage contained within boundaries as in plate 75. The undercut carving is a feature attributed to Yunnan pieces. A deep foot is ridged horizontally. The foundation is tin edged with brass. A related subject is on a box attributed to the early fifteenth century and concerns two chess players so absorbed in the game that trees grew up about them (Low Beer, 1950). Despite the Wanli style border, the unusual use of spun rather than hammered metal points to a late date. Probably late eighteenth-century. Diameter 15 cm, depth 7.2 cm.
Private collection

lustrated by Lee Yu-kuan (1972: Pl. 98) but the rim does not appear on other than Yunnan pieces. The most remarkable of the Yunnan subjects are the 'insect' dishes. Garner illustrated one from a private collection (1979: Pl. 74); there is a box in the BASF collection, Munster, with the same design (Strasser, 1988: Pl. 7); and another in the Fitzwilliam Museum, Cambridge *(Pl. 83)*. Yet another virtually identical box is in the Palace Museum at Beijing (Palace Museum, 1985: Pl. 154) and there is still another in Beijing with a guri border on the side (*ibid*: Pl. 156) All have the same confusion of insects and small reptiles, among them a remarkable praying mantis, variously disposed in a crowded pattern. I know of six with virtually the same design; probably there are others.

There is another type that may be from Yunnan for it is certainly the product of some outland factory. The box in plate 82 has a peculiar snail-like squiggle as a sky diaper. This unattractive feature is found also in plates 67, 70 and 71 in the Lee Family Collection (Lee King Tsi, 1990) and on some pieces of Kangxi porcelain. In the same collection (Lee King Tsi: Pl. 66) is a rectangular tray with a number of unusual and barbaric features which may very well be from the same source. On the strength of Kangxi porcelain I am inclined to attribute them to the very end of the Ming, but the Lees call them 'Ming 16th century'.

How are the majority of 'Yunnan' pieces to be dated? Low Beer said 'probably 16th century' and Garner left out the probably. It is best left at that until some positive evidence is produced.

Between the last days of Wanli and the first of Qianlong there are a hundred and seventeen years and the only credible marked piece in all that time is the porcelain-bodied Kangxi vase in plate 89.

With the empire in turmoil, the provinces in rebellion and a foreign invader keeping up constant pressure, it would be reasonable to think that the sophisticated arts of the court would not flourish. Nevertheless, there are a few ceramic objects of both the last reigns. Probably little enough lacquer was made, but specialist craftsmen could not suddenly turn their hands to something else, and no doubt here and there lacquer workshops in the provinces kept up some sort of production.

A possible candidate for the declining years of the Ming is that group of lacquers I have called 'Sichuan'. They are distinctive although there is a relationship to the usual Yunnan type. Plate 86 with a squirrel-like creature in a grape-vine, and plate 85 with a large cricket among melons are related to the more ambitious 'Insect Boxes', and they have other common features as well.

The close patterning against a plain ground, the crowded and involuted design, and a recognisable degree of undercutting all point to Yunnan. A third box of this type is in the Národní Museum of Prague where Dr. Cerná of that museum asserts that it was made in Beijing by workers imported from Sichuan. This seems likely and justifies distinguishing the group as 'Sichuan lacquers'. Sichuan, after all, borders Yunnan. A fourth piece, identifiably of the same type, although the subject matter differs, is shown in plate 87. This has a Wanli type of flower-trail along the sides. All four are lacquered in a distinctive brown-red and three of the four have a metal rim to both cover and box. The group may have been produced in the reigns of Tianqi (1621–27) and Chongzhen (1628–44), but a late eighteenth- or nineteenth-century date is also possible.

One piece of lacquer bearing the reign mark of Tianqi is known, it is a large lidded vase in dark brown lacquer, moulded and appliquéd in rough emulation of carving. Although moulded lacquer is known to have been applied to vessels during the Tang, the method was dropped in favour of the more expensive and arduous technique of carving. It would not have been unnatural for the practice to have enjoyed fresh life in the troubled years when costs had to be cut; or even that the craft persisted in some remote provincial workshops. There is, for example, an attractive, moulded bowl in Stuttgart.

A lidded box with a Chongzhen reign mark (Lee, 1972: Pl. 135) is impressed and appliquéd in a similar manner to the Tianqi vase. Another, from the same workshop, also bears the Chongzhen mark in an ornamental cartouche *(Pl. 88)*. I have seen other lidded vases with this mark and two smaller unmarked ones from the same factory. A lidded box is in the British Museum (Garner, 1979: Pl. 95) which Garner called eighteenth-century but he did not mention that it had a seal mark of Wanli on the base; the museum calls it nineteenth-century but it was in fact made in the Ryukyu Islands, perhaps in the seventeenth century. The inserted circle in the fourteenth-century vase-stand in plate 5 is of the same type, although the stand is three centuries earlier.

Although the moulded method lacks the precision of true carved lacquer, these pieces have a certain clumsy breadth that is refreshing when set against the meticulous carving and sharp colour of typical Qing pieces. But when and where were they made? Garner claimed to have seen such pieces with marks of Xuande, Chenghua, Zhengde and Wanli, and mentioned that one bearing the Chongzhen mark was known, probably the piece illustrated by Lee Yu-kuan. All these, with the possible exception of the British Museum piece and a

Plate 88 a, b **Vase**

There is a Chongzhen reign mark in a floral cartouche 3 cm above the base. The russet-coloured lacquer is moulded, impressed and applied. Although the foundation is possibly wood, the base is thick earthenware and may be original. Possibly the construction of so large a vase at that date was difficult, or it may be a clumsy repair. The workmanship is coarse but the vase has a strong barbaric presence. There exists a hexagonal box of the same workshop with a similar reign mark (Lee, 1972). Others with a like technique are to be found with a Tianqi mark. Are these strange pieces the work of a distinctive provincial atelier of their ostensible date? Or are they, as is more generally thought, late Qing? Height 46 cm, diameter 17 cm.
Private collection

not very typical dish in Copenhagen that he conceded might be eighteenth-century, Garner consigned to the late nineteenth or early twentieth centuries. They may be. The late seventeenth-century shapes suggest that they might have been made at that time in some remote centre that regretted the defeat of the native dynasty and chose the fiction of its continuance. Was that centre Yunnan, through which the last Ming pretender retreated on his way to Burma? Some insist that these pieces are quite modern. If so, evidence should be readily available, but none has yet been advanced. If they are no more than modern fakes is it not curious that the faker should have chosen such insignificant reign marks rather than the more prestigious ones of earlier emperors? Was it not that Tianqi and Chongzhen were names still fresh in the memory? If they are, in fact, of the late nineteenth or the twentieth century, it is clear that they were never seriously intended to fake carved lacquer, but rather to satisfy customers who required what today would be called an 'antique finish'. Nor are the best of them entirely unsuccessful. The reign-marks are best disregarded. The distinctive red-brown of the lacquer is precisely the shade of the 'Sichuan' group.and there can be little doubt that, whether of the late seventeenth century or the early twentieth century, Sichuan is where they were made. Apart from these moulded vases which, whatever

their place and date of origin, are oddities, there must have been carved lacquer from the fading years of the Ming. It is beyond belief that between the death of Wanli and the advent of Qianlong no lacquer was made, yet one marked piece is known — the Kangxi porcelain vase lacquered with a guri pattern *(Pl. 89)* already mentioned above. Some, at least, of the last Ming pieces have probably been subsumed under the general heading of 'Wanli'.

CHAPTER 14

EARLY QING WARE

No marked lacquer of the first three Qing emperors is known. In the case of Shunzhi (1644–61) this could be expected, as his reign covered the unsettled years of conquest. Marked ceramic pieces of the reign do exist but the disorganisation that followed the subversion of the Ming empire was not likely to have been conducive to the cultivated arts. More surprisingly, there are no marked pieces for Kangxi (but see *Pl. 89*) when they might well be expected since it is recorded that in 1680 a lacquer workshop was again set up in the Forbidden City. The relocation of a lacquer factory in Beijing at that time supports the view that lacquer production there had virtually ceased either after the death of Wanli in 1619 or after the suicide of Chongzhen. A period of close on eighty years without marked lacquer is not an indication that lacquer had ceased to be made, but that it had ceased to be marked and as the great majority of lacquer of any period was not marked we should not be altogether surprised. We have therefore to fill this gap with what one hopes are intelligent guesses. Unfortunately, because of the over-emphasis that Garner and other collectors gave to early fifteenth-century lacquers, the different qualities of the Qing have been largely ignored and little study of eighteenth- and nineteenth-century wares has been attempted.

The alien dynasty from beyond the Great Wall, the Manchu, adopted a tolerant attitude to the culture of the empire they had conquered and many characteristics of the late Ming will have carried over into the early Qing, but as yet no equivalent to the ceramic 'traditional' style has been isolated. It may have been some years before there was any stylistic new departure. Probably there was a tendency to cling to accustomed Ming models and an incentive to reproduce antique types. Were some of the doubtful Yongle and Xuande pieces made in a spirit of national loyalty under Kangxi, a sort of silent rejection of a conquering regime? If so, it would help to explain some puzzling features in pieces doubtfully attributed to the early fifteenth century.

The only piece of identifiable Kangxi carved lacquer so far known, a vase in the Palace Museum, Beijing (*Pl. 89*), is built around a marked porcelain body and can be accepted as of the period. It is an important clue for it implies that large porcelain shapes may help us to fill the Kangxi gap and shows that some other guri ware may be expected. It is a reasonable guess — since this vase is based on porcelain probably manufactured in Jingdezhen — that it should be dated before 1680, the year in which the government lacquer workshop was re-established in Beijing.

If the porcelain influence initially came from the south, a tendency to copy the more spectacular shapes of porcelain and bronze moved north with the lacquerers. In certain collections, there are several handsome vases called Qing of which some at least may be from early in the dynasty although one pair is dated as late as 1784 (*Pl. 109*). Others have the over-florid appearance of the nineteenth century and are more likely to have been created for the Dowager Empress Cixi whose marble boat on the lake side of the Summer Palace is a monument to her taste.

One might expect, by analogy with developed Kangxi porcelain, that there would have been a return to bright colours and the use of green in lacquer but there seems little evidence for it, although some Qing lacquers do have a dark green ground. It is probable that throughout the late seventeenth and eighteenth centuries settled conditions under Kangxi allowed provincial lacquer centres to flourish but that at first there was no lead from a disinterested court to stamp its style upon the period. A transitional style should be looked for among pieces that have some of the qualities of Wanli, the last Ming emperor whose lacquers we certainly know, and of Qianlong whose reign marks on lacquer are not uncommon and whose styles are well-established.

Colonel Strange (1926) whose book is insufficiently known, attributed several pieces to Kangxi of which one, the magnificent table in Stuttgart, is surely mid-fifteenth century, and two others which modern opinion would not hesitate to attribute to Qianlong. For the rest there is no evidence that they are Kangxi although they may be. Coromandel screens and a flat lacquer screen made for the Austrian Emperor Leopold I are indisputably of the period but are only marginally helpful when considering carved lacquer. They do at least serve to show the range of subject and decoration that may be expected.

Of greater importance is the handsome black, red and brown table in plate 90. It is soundly constructed and the handling of colour, the subtle red tinge inside the pavilions, the varied impact of the red in sea and air, is admirable. The carving of the diapers of undulating waves and square florets is good. The well-designed landscape is framed in a tendril of flowers that could well be Wanli; the side of the table-top is a linked swastika diaper also to be found in Wanli but otherwise rare until the Qing; a further ribbon is a classic scroll interrupted with isolated flowers, and below that is a repeating pattern of angled petals, both Wanli features. For the broad floral pattern on the apron it is less easy to find a close seventeenth-century parallel. The lac-

Plate 89 **Porcelain-bodied Vase**
There is a Kangxi mark on the body. No other marked lacquer of this reign is known. It is, of course, possible that the lacquer is not contemporary with the mark. Kangxi? Height 44 cm.
Palace Museum, Beijing

quering is on three levels — black, red and brown. The brown is exposed only for the earth diaper; the background of the remainder, whether diapered or plain, is an extraordinary red that is not found on Ming pieces, and the black has a mirror-like quality. The underside is bright black scattered with gold leaves and flowers, randomly, much as on the margins of coromandel screens of the period.

This table not only has good grounds for being considered a link between Wanli and Qianlong, but its fine quality also suggests that it may well have been made at the freshly invigorated factory at Beijing soon after 1680. Clearly from the same factory is a large and fine three-piece screen in the Ethnological Museum in Vienna which is there regarded — correctly in my view — as Kangxi. I cannot agree with the opinion (Clunas, 1991) that this is in any way connected with the Qianlong Throne in the Victoria and Albert Museum. That throne may well have been made in Nanjing by specialist lacquer carvers whereas the screen and table

(Pl. 90) were probably the work of general carvers in Beijing who were able to work in ivory, tortoiseshell and wood with equal facility.

Another table, the small one in Frankfurt *(Pl. 91)*, although quite different in decoration, is surely Kangxi. In fact we are unlikely to be able to identify any single characteristic or group of characteristics belonging to the reign but rather must rely on a general perception — that a piece is not Ming, yet neither does it fit with any of the more easily recognised and identifiable types of Qianlong. Archaisms are likely to be common in all three of the first Qing reign periods, but I am inclined to accept that the more vigorous of the archaic type vases are Kangxi and the more mechanical ones are from the reign of his grandson.

Inevitably, there are grey areas. What, for example, is to be made of the attractive covered 'Peach Tree Box' in plate 93? The carving of leaves and fruit is more rounded and fluent than on Wanli pieces and the gnarled branches are carefully observed and well-

shaped into the body. It is conceived more sculpturally than is customary with Qianlong and the colour has more of the richness of the Ming than the sharpness of the Qing. At present the only certain evidence we have of the reign of Yongzheng (1723–35) comes from a couch-throne in Beijing which was presented to the Emperor by the Superintendent of the Imperial Silk Manufactory at Nanjing in 1729 (Zhu Jiajin, 1988). The rounded full-bodied carving of this magnificent piece is not unlike that of the 'Peach Tree Box' and the 'Lion Box' in plate 105. It is clear that carving of this type is to be attributed to the factories of the Yangtze basin, probably to Nanjing itself rather than to Beijing where lacquer workers concentrated on uncarved pieces.

If we can accept the 'Peach Tree Box' as Yongzheng we may also give 'The 'Plain' Princess Box' (Pl. 94) to the same reign. The border of fruit cannot be paralleled in known Qianlong pieces, and the gnarled stems, although on a much smaller scale, have something of the same well-shaped quality.

Plate 90 a, b Low Table **(kang)**
This important table helps to fill the gap between the last dated carved lacquer of Wanli and the earliest dated piece of Qianlong. The clouds are of the narrow form found in Jiajing landscapes, the sky is of an irregular elongated parallel pattern, the waves are undulating, and the earth diaper is a diagonally set floret in a double square. The extensive scene and the borders can be paralleled in Wanli lacquer and all proclaim late Ming. However, the distinctive colour and the obtrusion of the knees beyond the table-top suggest Qing, although a table dated 1573 in Tokyo (Riddell, 1979: Pl. 165) has this feature. The quality of this piece, taken with the elaboration of the underside, supports a late seventeenth-century date and a provenance from the revived imperial factory in Beijing. Kangxi. Early 1680s. Length 89 cm, width (excluding knees) 54 cm, height 34.3 cm.
Private collection

Li Hongqing referred to the lacquer of Qianlong as being left with unpolished edges, so that the general appearance has a sharpness and lack of mellowness that persists even when the piece is polished with wax. 'The colour of Ming lacquer,' he wrote, 'was red with a slightly purple tinge whereas the red of Qing wares was vivid but dull' (1957). Although this is generally true, the reds of the Ming are not all of one tone and hue, nor are the reds of Qianlong. Chemical analysis has shown that synthetic cinnabar first appeared in the early seventeenth century and that the dull dark red, which under Wanli is so often used as a foil for a brighter one, is created by the use of red iron oxide (haematite). Although considerable advances have been made in scientific analysis of lacquering materials, we are still a long way short of establishing criteria for accurate dating. The variations in depth of tone and intensity of hue are so great, and possible causes of variation so wide-ranging, that it is not probable that the scientist will ever be able to replace the connoisseur in this field — for which we may be thankful. Nor must it be forgotten that the relacquering of the surface of a piece may be done at any time after the carving.

The earliest dated example of Qianlong lacquer, 1746, is a bowl in the Victoria and Albert Museum (Pl. 95). Other similarly dated versions exist, which suggests that they may have been a set or, since they bear a poem by the Emperor, that they were made as presents for courtiers, rather like a signed photograph. It is indeed 'vivid but dull', a colour that is common in Qianlong although a group of lacquers associated with a dish dated 1787 in the same museum is reddish-brown. Plate 96 show a dish of the type. The carving of the cup is sharp and precise but that of the dish is less exact and more

Plate 92 a, b Hexagonal Four-tiered Box
Black lacquer over muted red. The top carved with a family scene of an infant being bathed in a tub watched by a Pekinese dog. The background of small florets is edged with clouds, rocks and foliage. The sides are carved with trails of flowers which are not precisely repeated on the different tiers. The foot is delicately carved with semi-florets in triangles. The black throughout has a high gloss. There are similarities, despite the scale, with the table in plate 90. Kangxi. Height 9.5 cm, width 10.2 cm.
Private collection

Plate 91 **Small Table**
This fine table, the top carved with two phoenixes in a close background of leaves and rocks, shows the eclectic character of the early Qing lacquers. Kangxi. Length 38.2 cm, width 25.7 cm, height 14.3 cm.
Museum für Kunsthandwerk, Frankfurt am Main

Plate 93 **The Peach Tree Box**
Red lacquer of one shade throughout over hard grey composition upon a wooden foundation. Interior and base lacquered brown. A beautifully designed peach tree springs from an attractive and unusual representation of the earth low down by the rim. The gnarled trunk is rounded into the background of a square-in-square diaper. The narrow foot-rim has a running key pattern. The subject and the controlled freedom of the drawing suggest a parallel with the porcelain of Yongzheng. Yongzheng. Diameter 18 cm, depth 9.5 cm.
Private collection

hurried. The dish is a rather ill-informed attempt at reproducing a Xuande style. It has a foliate edge and a fairly standard landscape, but the edge is bound with pewter and there is a brass rim to the base. It was not intended as a forgery for it bears a strongly carved reign mark within a rectangular cartouche, but was aimed rather at a popular taste for the 'antique'. A more modest example from the same period, and presumably the same factory, is a rectangular box with a crowded landscape, floral sides in the trailing manner of Wanli, and a discreditable scratched reign mark on the damaged base.

Garner sought to show from the two dated pieces in the Victoria and Albert Museum a deterioration in technique symptomatic of a disastrous decline in the art. This was unjustified. The carving on the well-known throne in the same museum (Strange, 1925: Pls. 10, 11), which has been dated to about 1777 by Craig Clunas on historical grounds, may be tediously over-decorated but it is not technically incompetent. Very much better is the work on the boxes in plate 98, the sides of which are carved with opposed five-clawed dragons amongst close-packed clouds above a line of large humpbacked waves of a type found in many Qianlong pieces. The tops show similar dragons on either side of a rectangular cartouche containing inscriptions. At the base of the cartouche is a tripartite rock rising from waves, a familiar feature of Jiajing and Wanli lacquer but rare in Qianlong. The carving is meticulous but not deep and there is no contrasting tone of red. The interiors are black. These boxes were made to store scrolls painted by court artists in 1776 and although the event they illustrated, the Emperor's 'Southern Progress', took place in 1751 the boxes are likely to have been made when the scrolls were painted.

An even later piece is a large panel of a mountainous landscape through which marches the victorious army of General Agui reducing as it goes the massive stone forts of rebellious magnates *(Pl. 99).* The carving is in vermilion against a background of blue, brown and green. A large cartouche bears a long description de-

Plate 96 a, b **Dish**

Edged with pewter. The reverse is carved with Buddhist emblems
and a Qianlong reign mark in a square cartouche. It is of the same
date and factory as an inscribed dish dated 1781 in the Victoria and
Albert Museum. The carving is deep and the edges sharp. Bracket-
lobed dishes with pewter edges vary in quality. They usually bear a
large Qianlong mark on a metal inset on the reverse and were
probably a commercial product made for export to other Asian
countries or for the cheaper end of the market. They might be
thought to be late Qing were it not for the dated example.
Qianlong. Diameter 33.5 cm.
Private collection

Plate 97 **Buddhist Altar Ornament**
Red and black over a dull yellow which is responsible for the green quality of the black. The form derives from a reliquary (Nara National Museum, 1982: Pls. 56, 57). Similar ornaments are known in metal and porcelain but this lacquer example seems to be unique. Possibly Kangxi. Height 16 cm, diameter of base 10.5 cm.
Private collection

Plate 98 **Pair of Scroll Boxes**
Boxes of this type were made to store imperial scrolls painted by court artists. These are inscribed as containing paintings nos. 7 and 8 of the Qianlong Emperor's Southern Tour. The series would originally have numbered twelve (see also Moss, 1983: Pl. 146). Although the tour of the south took place in 1751, the scrolls were painted in 1776 and the boxes were probably made at that time. The quality is fine and the contrast in colour and carving between these imperial pieces and the commercial Qianlong product such as the 1787 dish in the Victoria and Albert Museum is great. Qianlong. Length 75.7 cm, width 16.7 cm, depth 16.7 cm.
Spink & Son Ltd

Plate 99 **Landscape Panel**
A memorial panel showing the campaigns of General Agui who was sent in 1771 to suppress an uprising in the mountains of Sichuan. The rebels surrendered in 1776. Agui was personally greeted by the Qianlong Emperor on his return to Beijing and it is reasonable to suppose this magnificent panel was commissioned at the time. Qianlong. Length 77.5 cm, width 9.25 cm.
Spink & Son Ltd

probably in Sichuan, and certainly for an unsophisticated market.

A distinctive group of late Qianlong lacquers is represented by a twelve-sided dish loaded with Sanskrit inscriptions in the Linden Museum, Stuttgart *(Pl. 100)* dated 1775; a begging bowl with gilded brass lion-head handles *(Pl. 101)*, which has a heavy brass base engraved with pseudo-mantras in a passable imitation of Tibetan script; another begging bowl with similar handles in the Asian Art Museum of San Francisco; and yet another bowl of similar shape but without handles and carved with seven Buddhas in Beijing (Palace Museum, 1985: Pl. 354). A square tray on a brass core in the BASF Museum *(Pl. 102)*, has a heavy brass inset on the reverse cast with a Qianlong seal mark, which relates it to plate 101. The dramatic swirling drapery of the figures on this tray connects it in turn with the round unmarked box in plate 103 on which an elaborate landscape is very deeply carved into a dull red body through a full red surface. The reverse has a handsome phoenix among flowers and the sides are covered with a close design of hawthorn blossoms. It is perhaps as deeply carved a piece of lacquer as exists. The clue to this generally neglected group lies in the inscription on the shoulder of the begging bowl in plate 101, which reads: 'Qianlong Department of Manufacture', clearly a commercial operation.

scribing the campaign. As the capture of the rebel strongholds was completed in 1776, it can be assumed that the panel was made after the General's triumphant return to Beijing. The deterioration would indeed have had to be sudden between this and the dish in the Victoria and Albert Museum of ten years later , but we are not comparing like with like. The boxes and the panel were made for the Emperor whereas the red-brown dishes *(Pl. 96)* were possibly made for export,

Although on the evidence of the 1787 dish we can attribute most of these red-brown lacquers to the last ten years of Qianlong, it is possible that the two distinct types, the red-brown deeply carved and the bright vermilion, were made throughout the reign in different workshops. There is no reason to suppose that a universal style prevailed throughout the empire.

Several features are characteristic of Qianlong lacquer although not necessarily peculiar to that reign alone. The designs are often over-full because intricacy gave proof of high skill, laborious workmanship and great expense. The result is often an impression of jewelled richness *(Pl. 104)* but sometimes of mere confusion and lack of clarity. Decorative shapes are often rectangular, which is rare in Ming. Rocks are normally wrinkled to suggest texturing. Often pavilions and rocks are edged

with a long trail of leaves as though with ivy. Other common characteristics are the formal framing of a landscape with a double ribbon in various designs *(Pls. 106, 107)*. The trick of rendering a tumult of waves, first but rarely seen in Xuande *(Pl. 45)*, becomes commonplace under Qianlong. It is always fine and effective *(Pl. 105)*.

Large circular boxes with polychrome carving are typical of imperial wares intended as birthday gifts to high court officials *(Pl. 106)*. More modest routine pieces which gain from their modesty, such as the landscape box in plate 107, are in the same tone of cinnabar throughout. The much finer and more imaginative

Plate 100 **Twelve-sided Box**
There is a Sanskrit inscription containing the date 1775. Qianlong.
Length 27.7 cm, depth 8.1 cm.
Linden-Museum, Stuttgart

Plate 101 a, b **Begging Bowl**
Inscribed on the shoulder is 'Qianlong, Department of
Manufacture'. The heavy brass base is engraved with pseudo-
mantras in Tibetan script. A similar bowl is in San Francisco, and a
bowl of this shape is in Beijing (Palace Museum, 1985: Pl. 354).
Qianlong. Diameter 36 cm, depth 19 cm.
Spink & Son Ltd

landscape on the lid of the fan-shaped box in plate 108 is in a more subdued red closer to that of the Ming. It is perhaps Kangxi. The most interesting and best carved lacquers are the well-observed landscapes that illustrate some rural activity such as planting and harvesting. The best of these are quite unlike the romantic landscapes of the late fifteenth century, 'the cloud-capped towers, the gorgeous palaces'. They are more complex, more Western, more realistic and less universal, but lively and charming.

The view that there was an immediate deterioration in the last years of Qianlong and that the art was in terminal decline through the remainder of the dynasty is contradicted by two pieces, a brush holder in Beijing (Pl. 112), and a box in the Fitzwilliam Museum (Pl. 114), both Jiaqing (1796–1820). The technical quality of these pieces is not less than in many a piece made in the preceding reign. Over-fanciful pieces, such as in plate 115 ('miracles of misapplied ingenuity' as was said of certain Japanese ceramics), are not uncommon and may well be from the mid-nineteenth century. Another type which I should be happy to call Daoguang is represented by a rather flattened spherical box on a lead base (Pl. 116). Some of this sort bear evident signs of the use of a drill. In Beijing they are called 'late Qing' (Palace Museum, 1985: Pls. 383, 384).

The Jiaqing and Daoguang pieces discussed so far are, of course, fairly straightforward continuations of standard Qianlong lacquers and display little individual quality. Quite different are the pieces illustrated in plates 117 and 118, the work of named artists of the mid-nineteenth century. Lu Guisheng (c. 1780–1850) signed four very attractive red lacquer panels (Moss, 1983) of which one is shown in plate 117. The carving is shallow but precise; the scenes are more open and in-timately observed than is normal; and the small appropriate diapers make for a distinctively textured ground. Lu Guisheng is said also to have carved figures in the round. That being so, plate 123 may possibly also be his work.

It seems that Lu Guisheng's influence was considerable and may have persisted throughout the century. Plate 118 shows another panel, this time by Sun Guoxin (Moss 1986), clearly a contemporary of Lu Guisheng on whose work it shows an advance in certain respects. The brilliant representation of water and the dramatically contrasted patterning of the lutanist's dress is finer than anything in the Lu Guisheng panels. The influence of these two masters in its decadence is probably to be seen in the square trays in plate 119 as well as in the hinged box of plate 120, which must date from the end of the nineteenth or the beginning of the twentieth century.

W. Winkworth, in an ill-advised aside about Qing lacquers in general, wrote: 'this sort of thing fulfils very well... the function of looking expensive. But it must not be mistaken for art' (1935). All that he was saying was that they did not look like the fourteenth- and fifteenth-century wares which, at the time that he wrote, were the only ones to be praised. Qing lacquers do not pretend to the merits of the Yuan or early Ming — which one may quite reasonably prefer — but they have their own merits. They should be seen as more akin to jewellery than to painting. The refinement of detail and the exploitation of technical skill is not the highest art, but at least what the Qing lacquer-masters set out to do they did at times very well. And if sometimes they overstepped the border into vulgar opulence it is no more than has happened at almost all periods of intense artistic creativity.

Plate 102 a, b **Tray**
Lacquered red on a brass foundation. There is a Qianlong seal mark on a brass inset. The front is decorated with the 'Island of the Genii', showing immortals and boy servants in a large palace garden. Ivy hangs down the rock faces. Qianlong. Length 33.9 cm, width 33.9 cm, depth 2.8 cm.
BASF Lacquer Museum, Munster

Plate 103 **Double-sided Box**
Extremely deep (6 mm) carving cuts through a thin full-red surface into a dark-red base. The interior is black. The swirling drapery of the figures relates to plates 101 and 102. The underside is carved with a phoenix among peonies. The sides of both box and lid are thickly covered with plum blossoms and tendrils of foliage. Qianlong. Diameter 15.5 cm, depth 11.5 cm.
Private collection

Plate 104 **Four-lobed Trinket Box**
An exact duplicate is in the National Palace Museum, Taibei. Qianlong. Length 12.2 cm, width 9.8 cm, depth 5 cm.
Private collection

Plate 105 **Lion Box**
Four lions disport themselves amongst crested waves. It was a favourite Qing device to show dragons and other beasts amidst a tumble of waves. There are eleven examples of this type of scene in Beijing (Palace Museum, 1985) and four in Taibei (National Palace Museum, 1971). Some of these are probably Yongzheng or early in the reign of his successor. Yongzheng. Diameter 20.5 cm, depth 8.5 cm.
Private collection

*Plate 106 a, b **Polychrome Games Box***
This type of box is familiar, although not with its games content.
Two similar boxes are in Taibei (National Palace Museum, 1971),
one with a Jiajing mark, the other with a mark of Qianlong. Yet an-
other Qianlong-marked piece is in the Asian Art Museum of San
Francisco (San Francisco, 1986). The Jiajing piece is, as one would
expect, a deeper, duller red. Is this unmarked example perhaps
Kangxi? Diameter 37 cm, depth 10 cm.
Private collection

*Plate 107 a, b **The Deep Red Tazza***
Two shades of red on wood foundations, base lacquered black. It is reasonable to assume that this unusual, possibly unique shape derives from a European Christian chalice. Probably Kangxi. Height 19.5 cm, diameter of cup 21 cm, diameter of base 16 cm.
Private collection

Plate 108 **Fan-shaped Picnic Box**

Black interior and base. This is perhaps part of an ensemble made up of three boxes of similar shape and a central circular box. The figures are shaped well into the background but the foliage is carved vertically. The scene is not unlike official early Ming landscapes but is better spaced and the figures better observed. Qianlong. Length 37.5 cm, width 15.5 cm, depth 5.5 cm.
Private collection

Plate 109 **Pair of Vases**

Inscribed 'Imitating Antiquity' and dated 1784. The imitation is general rather than particular. The rectangular decoration and the square-in-square diaper are typical Qing features. A similar vase with a *gui*, a halberd-shaped pattern that was an emblem of office, is in Taibei (National Palace Museum, 1971). Qianlong. Height 28.5 cm.
British Museum

Plate 110 **Gift Box**
These small polychrome asymmetrical boxes, often shaped like fruit, were commonly grouped inside a much larger box and were probably intended for sweetmeats. Qianlong. Length 12 cm, width 8.4 cm, depth 4.3 cm.
Private collection

Plate 111 **Mountain Landscape Box**
Although in many ways a traditional upright landscape, this is
shown to be late by its greater naturalism and the unusually simple
sides. Probably early nineteenth-century. Length 18.7 cm, width
12.8 cm, depth 4.1 cm.
Náprstekovo Museum, Prague

Plate 112 **Red Brush-holder**
There is a seal dating to Jiaqing. The quality of this carving sufficiently disposes of the theory that by the end of Qianlong's reign
the craft was in terminal decline. Jiaqing. Diameter 10.3 cm,
height 15.2 cm.
Palace Museum, Beijing

*Plate 113 **Incense Box on Stand***
The carving is shallow but refined. The elegant base is like that in
plate 112. Qianlong or Jiaqing. Overall height 19 cm, width
23.5 cm.
Private collection

Plate 114 **Box**

The billowing crested waves are typical Qing. Among pieces at Beijing called mid-Qing six have identical frames while others have double ribbons of different design. The rectangular shape of the rocks is distinctive; pieces with similar rocks, grouped together, might help to establish a certain designer, atelier and date. Jiaqing. Diameter 47 cm.
Fitzwilliam Museum, Cambridge

Plate 115 **Bat-shaped Box**

A similar box is in the Victoria and Albert Museum. Called Kangxi by Strange, 1926. Jiaqing. Length 24.6 cm, width 11.7 cm.
Aberdeen City Art Gallery

Plate 116 **Box**

Lead base. These heavy boxes seem to have been made over a considerable period. Lee Yu-kuan illustrates one as Xuande: 'The lacquer is applied over a metal body which, from its excessive weight, may be gold' (1964: Pls. 3a, b). The same box is also called 'late sixteenth century', which is perhaps possible (Watson, 1981). The notion that such boxes may be upon a gold base arose from a misunderstanding of an early text that held that some lacquers were 'on gold'. It has been suggested that at a later time a heavy foundation was employed to imply the presence of a gold base. The plastic reproductions made by the National Palace Museum, Taibei, are also heavy but can be seen not to have been carved. Daoguang. Diameter 12.2 cm.
Private collection

Plate 117 **Panel: Painting Prunus**

Among rocks in the lower right corner is the seal of Lu Guisheng, a prolific and distinctive lacquer artist whose working life may have extended over the entire first half of the nineteenth century. Several signed pieces by Lu Guisheng are known and dated to the reign of Daoguang whereas others bear Qianlong marks. It is likely that some workshops continued to use the prestigious Qianlong mark for many years after it was appropriate, and these early marked pieces may not belong to the reign. Lu Guisheng is therefore more safely dated '*floreat* 1821–50'. According to Paul Moss (Moss, 1983, p. 210) Lu Guisheng made inkstone boxes, lacquered wrist-rests, solid lacquer images of Guanyin and large red carved lacquer objects such as pairs of six-fold screens and tables. An article in *Wenwu* 1957, vol. 7 refers. Daoguang. 55 cm by 60 cm.
Sydney L. Moss Ltd.

Plate 118 **Landscape with Lutanist**

The panel is integrated with the frame on a wood base. There is an engraved seal of Sun Guoxin in the bottom left corner and a carved seal in relief on the right. One other piece signed by the artist is recorded. It is suggested by Paul Moss (Moss, 1986), with good reason, that Sun must either have worked in the atelier of Lu Guisheng or been greatly influenced by him. The style of this very attractive panel is distinct, the representation of water, the decoration of the frame and the treatment of the musician's skirt are all unparalleled. Daoguang. 60.4 cm by 45.8 cm.
Sydney L. Moss Ltd.

Plate 119 **Pair of Trays**
The subjects, unusual in showing a single female figure in a landscape, perhaps show the influence of Japanese woodcuts of courtesans, which were popular at the time of Daoguang. It has been suggested that these may be by a follower of Lu Guisheng (see above). Although the flat expressive carving is similar, the quality of the present trays is not at all equal to the panels, which suggests that they are studio work. Nineteenth-century. Length 18 cm, width 18 cm.
Private collection

CHAPTER 15

THE LATE NINETEENTH CENTURY AND AFTER

Briefly, after the court returned to Beijing in 1870, from where it had fled ten years before when the British and French sacked the Summer Palace, there was a period of relative stability under the influence of the Dowager Empress Cixi who seized power from her weak son, Tongzhi. Although so far it has not been possible to identify any lacquer made at this time, it is likely that some of the most extravagant late Qing pieces were the last expression of the dynasty's delusions of grandeur. They are bright, big and heavily decorated. It may be that many of the extravagant pieces now seen in the West came from the Summer Palace, but they may equally have been looted after the capture of Beijing in 1900. After the Dowager Empress's nominal retirement in 1889 the collapse and disappearance of the Manchu was not long delayed.

If the nineteenth century has had little critical attention, the twentieth has had none. Throughout the last half of the nineteenth century the power of central government diminished, foreign incursions, banditry, internal rebellions and the encroachment of the Western powers, followed closely by Russian and Japanese aggression, impoverished and fragmented the country and resulted in its virtual partition. The Taiping Rebellion, the Opium Wars, the capture of Beijing, the flight of the Tongzhi Emperor, the sack of the Summer

Palace, the Boxer Rebellion, were not conducive to the production of lacquer of imperial quality. Although the seclusion of the Forbidden City dulled the sound of distant guns, even in that cloistered calm a shortage of money could not be concealed. But while there were still local magnates, warlords and wealthy landowners who were prepared to pay for it, lacquer never ceased to be made, although perhaps the class of cultivated scholars and connoisseurs, sustainers of refined taste, had been eliminated or impoverished. The workers in the lacquer factories continued to exist, they cut corners and did the job less well. We find elements of Qianlong decoration in decline, the diapers are reduced to their simplest diagrammatic form, and the flowers in the cartouches are degraded to barely recognisable symbols; yet a certain traditional skill persists.

That indefatigable lacquer scholar Lee Yu-kuan wrote of a lacquerer named Zhen Rizhu, who at the end of the nineteenth century opened a factory to produce high-quality lacquer wares. According to Lee (1972) his work was 'definitely more beautiful and stronger than those made in the Daoguang reign'. He added that many of them are still in existence and that his 'artistic style' had become a tradition. Unfortunately he illustrated no examples. Lee also referred to another artist, Lao Wei: 'unless one knows that an article was made by

*Plate 120 a, b **Boat-shaped Box with Hinged Lid***
The shallow, flat carving suggests that this came from the same
workshop as plate 117 but the carving is more delicate. The black
base originally bore the word CHINA. In 1891 the USA insisted that
all imported goods carry the name of the country of origin. It is
likely that this box dates from the first decade of the twentieth century, during the reign of one of the last Manchu emperors.
Xuantong. Length 16.5 cm, width 6.3 cm, depth 3.6 cm.
Private collection

Plate 121 **Pair of Vases**
Full rich red on a foundation of brass; the bases are enamelled
blue except for the rims. The carving is deep. A pair of vases of similar style and colour was marked 'The Peking Lacquer Production
and Co-operative Society, China'. I have not been able to find
when this Society operated; others may be luckier. The use of the
form 'Peking' eliminates the Guomindang (Republican,
Kuomintang) period during which the capital was known as
Beiping (Peiping). Xuantong or post-1948. Height 15.4 cm.
Private collection

Plate 122 **Two Vases**
These are typical of products made for the tourist trade. (b) was
probably made in the 1980s in Beijing, where a great many similar
articles are still being turned out. It has a metal core enamelled
blue. (a) is lighter in weight, the core is wood, the interior is lacquered dull black, the rims of base and top are brass, the carving is
less sharp than in (b) and there is more attempt at detail. All the
traditional devices are in a degraded and superficial form, and yet
it is interesting to see that in (a) the diapers are correctly used. No
lacquer vases are found before the reigns of Tianqi and
Chongzhen, and these are doubtful; the form became common
under the Qing emperors and has remained so. Twentieth-century.
Height (a) 15.5 cm, (b) 17.5 cm.
Private collection

him, it is very difficult to distinguish his twentieth-century works from old originals.' When Lee Yu-kuan suggested that Lao Wei should sign his excellent wares, the
reply was that foreigners would not pay a high enough
price for new pieces but would only buy them as Ming
or Kangxi and if they were in imperfect condition and
cracked, or if they were assured that they came from
one of the imperial palaces. The assurance was rarely
lacking and Lao Wei is reported to have been expert in
producing medium-sized cracks. It seems likely that
these fakes will all have been of Qing types.

I have come across only two marks that help us to date
the lacquers of the first half of the twentieth century.
The first, commonly seen on inferior cigarette boxes
and the like, is the simple word 'CHINA' written on the
base. This was in response to a United States law passed
towards the end of the nineteenth century that required the country of origin to be marked on all imported goods. It would certainly have been placed on
lacquer made for export at that date and though it is to
be found on some very inferior lacquer made today it
was perhaps not used in many of the intervening years.
The boat-shaped box in plate 120 once bore this mark
but it has been erased. The carving is unusually shallow
and delicate, the subject on the lid is original, but the
clumsy hinge detracts from such virtues as it has. It is
not without individuality and is probably the work of a
minor workshop in the tradition of Lu Guisheng (Moss,
1983: Pl. 147).

The other mark is more interesting. I have seen a pair
of vases inscribed under the base in English: 'Made by
Peking Lacquer Production and Co-operative Society,
China'. It should be possible to learn when this society
was formed but so far I have been unsuccessful. The
pair of vases in plate 121 are unmarked but were certainly the product of the co-operative at the same time
as the marked pieces. The five-clawed dragons might
lead one to suppose that they were made in the days of
the last emperor, say between 1900 and 1911. During
the Guomindang (Kuomintang) period Chiang Kai-
shek renamed the capital Beiping (Peiping) so we can
suppose that these vases were not made between 1928
and 1945, when the Communists captured the city and
it resumed its former name. The alternative, that they
were made in the 1950s, implies that the five-clawed
dragon had declined to a mere decorative feature designed to appeal to foreign buyers. A date before 1928
is probable.

The modern commercial lacquerer's favourite form is
the vase. The carving is usually deep, sharp-edged and
vertical. The colour is a sharp red, the body is often
metal that has been enamelled blue inside, and both

rim and base have an exposed edge of brass. Such pieces are made in great quantities in Beijing and may be bought in Friendship Stores all over China. The vase (b) in plate 122 was probably made in the past ten years, since the Gang of Four were overthrown. It has a pseudo-floral pattern on neck and shoulders, and the body is divided into cartouches by similar formal tendrils. Within the cartouches are naturalistic sprays of not clearly identifiable flowers and there is an elongated 'petal' ring around the base. Many of the same characteristics are repeated on the landscape vase (a) in the same plate but the carving is less deep, the colour less sharp and the symbolic tendrils and flowers have not been simplified to the same degree. It is light and seems to be on a wood foundation which has been covered with dull black lacquer on the inside. The border is even less like a row of petals than the border of the taller vase. The landscapes have been separated not by a formal cartouche but by the device of tall rocks outlined with ivy leaves. The diapers are of extreme diagrammatic simplicity. The landscape vase looks the earlier of the two but it is doubtful if it is more than thirty years old. The colour of the waisted dragon vases in plate 121 is richer and darker than in these later vases and the wave diaper of carefully carved undulations is surprisingly good. If the dragon vases are of the turn of the century, while China was still nominally imperial, it shows how little commercial work had altered in nearly 100 years.

There are vases and boxes now appearing in startling black and red, a formula first seen in the late fifteenth century, and I have seen one in strident yellow. Recently a number of trays and dishes have descended on the curio shops and antique markets which have been drenched in a peculiarly unpleasing deep red as though coated with raspberry jam, no doubt with the intention of repeating the deep reds of the early Ming. Perhaps they are evidence of the commercial enterprise of Taiwan or Korea. Hopefully they represent the nadir of carved lacquer; from this point on only improvement is possible.

The National Palace Museum in Taiwan has been responsible for reproductions of its own Ming and Qing lacquers in plastic. They are accurate, cast from moulds, but are a good deal heavier than the originals and the surface quality is too uniformly suave. A cursory glance shows that they are homogeneous and not

Plate 123 God of Longevity
Red lacquer on a partly carved solid wood foundation. Very fine quality. Is this perhaps from the atelier of Lu Guisheng who is known to have carved solid figures? The hands are replacements. Mid-Qing. Height 46 cm.
Private collection

layered. They are no longer made and examples consequently are of some interest. Plastic is, after all, no more than lacquer's shameless descendant.

Very different are the vast pieces of fantastic elaboration, lions, elephants, huge vases, lidded pots of alarming dimensions, screens to dazzle the eye, fit only for the foyers of modern luxury hotels or the palaces of oil sheikhs. They are to be seen in Shanghai and are probably made, if not there, elsewhere in the Yangtze valley. They are usually of over-bright vermilion lacquer laid on a carved wooden core. The surface of the best of them is closely carved in a sharp, superficially competent manner.

These pieces raise the question whether all Chinese lacquering over carved wood is modern. Carved wood was lacquered over 2,000 years ago, but when was the method resumed in more recent times? The carving of the cheerful God of Longevity in plate 123 is fine. It probably dates from the middle of the nineteenth century and may be the work of Lu Guisheng.

So far modern lacquer has not found a distinctive voice. Somewhere between the mass tourist market and the palatial monstrosities to be seen in the Friendship Stores there is room for a revival. Chinese craftsman, with all their traditional manipulative skills and patience, are available; what is lacking are the discerning and critical patrons who have the means to pay for fine contemporary works. The best lacquer has always provided objects of high luxury as well as a field for connoisseurship.

CHAPTER 16

ASSOCIATED LACQUERS OF ASIA

Collectors inevitably come across strange pieces of lacquer which, while clearly of a Chinese type, seem not to be Chinese. Often they are of little merit but are not for that reason of little interest. They have their place in the story. When, where, how and why, were they made?

The vast empire of China, not unlike the British empire, sent the ripples of its culture out into the adjacent world. As China was a great trading nation its influence was not limited to those countries with which it had a land frontier.

Japan learnt the art of lacquering from China. The earliest Japanese lacquer wares of any significance are thought to date from the seventh century. Carved lacquer had arrived in Japan by the last quarter of the thirteenth century, by way of the monk Xu Ziyuan. An inventory of 1367 lists a number of Chinese pieces in the possession of the Regents of Kamakura. The most influential import from China must have been in the early years of the Muromachi period (1392–1568) when gifts of carved lacquer were made by the Yongle Emperor to the shogun on five separate occasions between 1403 and 1434. The fact that carved lacquer was an acceptable and valued gift suggests that to the Japanese it was a rarity. May it not also follow that these gifts were not

sent after 1434 because, with their usual facility, the Japanese had learned the technique and were making carved lacquer themselves? It has been argued that since the Japanese could obtain it so readily from China there was no point in their making it, but that does not seem consistent with their national character.

It is said that a lacquer-master named Monnyu was the first Japanese to make carved lacquer (Garner, 1979). He flourished in the second half of the fifteenth century but nothing is known of what he made. Indeed, if he confined himself to copying Chinese pieces it is possible — since the Japanese were such meticulous copyists — that his work may never be distinguished from the originals. There was also a school of lacquer artists, said to have originated in the fifteenth century, that adopted the Japanese form of the combined names of the two famous Chinese lacquerers Yang and Cheng but none of their work before the nineteenth century has been identified. Low Beer believed that a number of the bird-and-flower dishes that Garner called Yuan were Japanese seventeenth-century copies and he went on to argue that there were 'far more Japanese carved lacquers than anyone could say'. The difference that Low Beer pointed to — a certain lack of calculated coherence in design that he called 'un-Chinese' — was, surely, a very un-Japanese characteristic also.

The mainstream of Japanese lacquer went another way. A distinctive type evolved which owed little to China. It was distinguished by the use of gold and silver and an astonishingly high finish. But there is one type of Japanese lacquer, known as kamakura-bori, in which instead of carving lacquer the wood is carved and then lacquered, a less time consuming business. The earliest known examples are said to date from the fourteenth century but most pieces seen today are nineteenth-century at the earliest and are often more recent. They are easily recognisable as the surface has been rubbed down so that highlights are darkened, as though carved lacquer had been eroded by wear. Originally, no doubt, this was intended as an 'antique finish' but, like so many techniques that begin as imitations, the pretence was given up and it developed an impetus of its own. More difficult are pieces where the wood is carved and red lacquer is evenly applied without the characteristic rubbing. In such cases one must be guided by the subject matter, or by some peculiarity of the drawing. The identifiable characteristics of good Japanese versions (or copies) of Chinese carved lacquer are first, a general appearance of over-meticulous and suave finish; secondly, a 'watered' appearance which cannot possibly be justified by honest wear; and thirdly, the use of a shape not appropriate to the subject. All these are evidenced in plate 125.

It is probable that if any supposed fourteenth- and fifteenth-century pieces turn out to be Japanese they will be amongst those that have an over-fluent design and excessive neatness and accuracy of workmanship. However, there are also some very boldly designed pieces that have so decidedly a Japanese flavour that they can hardly be doubted. Exquisitely carved *inro* are occasionally seen that argue a practised skill, but may they not have been made by Chinese craftsmen working in Japan?

The Ryukyu Islands, that half-way house between China, Korea and Japan, is best known for its mother-of-pearl lacquers. In the *Ge Gu Yao Lun* it is written 'that carved red lacquer is greatly favoured by peoples of Japan and the Ryukyu Islands', but no carved lacquer from the islands has been identified. The fearful bombardments of Okinawa during the Second World War may well have destroyed any that survived. If carved lacquer were made there we have no reason to believe it was exported for none has been recognised in Japan, where other Ryukyu types are treasured, and if any found their way to China they have been lost in the pool of Chinese lacquers.

There is, however, a distinctive Ryukyu type of which a few examples have surfaced. As with kamakura-bori it

Plate 124 ***Vase***
Red lacquer over carved wood. The carving is excellent but the two halves of the vase have sprung apart, perhaps when it was adapted to form a lamp. Possibly eighteenth-century. Height 24 cm, maximum diameter 10.5 cm.
Private collection

Plate 127 Small Treasure Box
Moulded and appliquéd on a wooden foundation. The red, brown and grey dragon is fitted exquisitely into the small space. The side of the box rises in what seems to be a typical Ryukyu fashion to frame the decoration on the lid. Both lid and box obtrude slightly where they meet. The inset base is lacquered black with a hint of brown. Ryukyu Islands. Probably eighteenth-century. Diameter 5.7 cm, depth 2.2 cm.
Mr Nicholas Harris

*Plate 125 **Japanese Incense Box***
The slightly domed lid, the extreme delicacy of the carving, the pose of the figure, the artificially induced appearance of 'watered silk' on the highlights in imitation of genuine wear such as that in plate 54, together with the mechanical precision of the key-fret around the side of the lid and box, combine to identify this as Japanese. Eighteenth- /nineteenth-century. Diameter 7.3 cm, height 2.8 cm.
Private collection

Plate 128 **Appliquéd Box**
Moulded lacquer applied to a wooden foundation. Lee Yu-kuan illustrates a trousseau chest of this type as 'between 1715 and 1750' (1972). An ornate box in the Malcolm Macdonald Collection at Durham University is described as Japanese. Ryukyu Islands. Eighteenth-century. Length 14.5 cm, width 11 cm, depth 4.7 cm.
Private collection

Plate 126 **Box**
The wooden core is decorated with a moulded and appliquéd three-clawed dragon clutching a pearl. The box stands on a broad encircling foot within which the base is inset. An identical box is in the Mikokai Collection (Itabashi Ward Museum, 1983). The way the dragon is accommodated tightly within the circular shape is not unlike an earthenware medallion of a phoenix in the National Museum of Korea. Ryukyu Islands. Probably eighteenth-century. Diameter 10.5 cm, depth 3.5 cm.
Private collection

Plate 129 **Black Octagonal Box**
The surface was shallowly carved or impressed when still malleable.
An example of a group with distinct characteristics that seems to
have developed at a distance from the mainstream and may derive
ultimately from the Song. The glossy black skin over a red under-
coat may be a clue to its antecedents, probably the Ryukyu Islands.
Perhaps eighteenth-century. Height 19 cm.
Dr Hu Shih-chang

Plate 130 **Black Tray**
The surface is a highly reflective dull black, appliquéd over a shallowly impressed background of diapers on a light wooden base.
Beyond the lobed frame is an almost solid mass of flowers and
leaves, the space between filled with dots. The outer edge of the
gallery is closely covered with formalised chrysanthemums. The reverse is sprinkled with gold spots, which suggests a Japanese source
such as the Ryukyu Islands. It is difficult to believe this is not from
the same source as plate 129. Probably eighteenth-century. Length
40.3 cm, width 23 cm, depth 2 cm.
Private collection

Plate 131 **Tray**
The grey composition body was moulded into shape while still malleable. The very thin red surface layer (which may be paint) is
much rubbed; the black reverse is covered with a land diaper. The
way the impressed decoration is accommodated to the space suggests the Ryukyu Islands. The beast is an unusual breed of Kylin.
Twentieth-century. Length 21 cm, width 16 cm.
Mrs Desmond North

arose from a wish to short-cut the process of creating a lacquer body deep enough to carve. A soft lacquer putty was cast in a shallow mould and when hardened was applied, rather like pastry shapes, to a flat-lacquered body. A circular box with a coiled dragon on the lid is illustrated, the only example of the type, in the catalogue of an exhibition of Ryukyu ware held in Tokyo in 1983 (Itabashi Ward Museum, 1983). I have two pieces from the same mould *(Pl. 126)*. A distinguishing feature of these boxes, which I have also seen on a plain lacquered box, is the broad continuous foot rim that surrounds a countersunk base; it appears on no other lacquer. These pieces are, presumably, eighteenth-century although there is really no reason why they should not be earlier. A small very attractive polychrome box in Mr Nicholas Harris's collection is in the same technique *(Pl. 127)*. The colours of the Harris box

lead on to the elaborate and attractive box in plate 128 which admirably fulfils the description 'Japanese in form but decorated with carved lacquer built up in thick layers by the use of lacquer putty, then coloured in a variety of shades of brown, yellow and green, as well as the more standard red' (Scott, 1984). There is another more elaborate example in the Malcolm Macdonald Collection in Durham, and Lee Yu-kuan illustrated a fine chest that he dated to the mid-eighteenth century (1972: Pl. 258). Others are illustrated in Itabashi Ward Museum (1987).

The typical lacquers of Thailand are not carved and bear little resemblance to the carved lacquers of China but there are two examples of a rather strange type that are certainly related to China and may be from Thailand. The clue is a box in the collection of Dr Hu

*Plate 132 **Carved Nut***
*Plate 132 **Carved Nut***
Very shallowly carved on a thin skin of nut over a pewter foundation. The wash of dull red over the brown of the nut is much
rubbed. The design suggests late seventeenth-century. Diameter
14 cm, depth 6.7 cm.
Private collection

Shih-chang of Hong Kong, acquired in Thailand where
it was credibly said to have been since the mid-nineteenth century *(Pl. 129)*. It is in black lacquer over a red
ground which shows through in the highlights not as a
calculated effect but due to natural wear. The relief is
very shallow and seems to have been achieved by tool-
ing into soft material rather than by carving. It is neat,
accurate and the drawing is expressive. The diapers for
earth, water and air are appropriate and not in the degraded late nineteenth-century form. Most of the ingredients of a typical Chinese landscape are there with the
exception of a pavilion. There is one token rock of the
pyramidal Jiajing/Wanli type but it has floated up from
the six o'clock position to the ten o'clock. Beyond the
circle that frames the landscape is a tooled pattern of
symbolic flower-shapes which spread over the edge to
meet a running key-fret. The body of the box is covered
closely with swirling flame-like arabesques that are not
remotely Chinese in character but seem to support an
attribution to Thailand.

Another piece from the same workshop is the tray in
plate 130. Once more the landscape is without buildings and there is only one small token rock. An earth
diaper is used inappropriately — clouds float against it.
Remarkably, the base is covered with brown/black lacquer sprinkled with gold dust in a Japanese way that
points to the Ryukyus.

A third piece, far inferior, a circular box in brown lacquer with a design of a bird against a background of
flower-like shapes, is coarsely and carelessly done with
little realisation of what the shapes are supposed to represent. It has a countersunk base rather in the manner
of the Ryukyu boxes but the foot rim is not so broad.
All three pieces are on wood and it is probable that the
lacquer used is not from *Rhus verniciflua*, which is not
indigenous to South East Asia, but from one of the several other species of *Rhus* that are lacquer-yielding.

The box and tray are attractive and interesting because
they show what can happen to Chinese carved lacquer
when it becomes naturalised in other lands. From time
to time other pieces turn up that excite attention because of their idiosyncrasies rather than their merits.
The tray in plate 131 seems to have been made by shaping a bastard lacquer body while it was still malleable;
the whitish-grey body was then clumsily tooled with a
strange Kylin against a background of a freely drawn
wave diaper. The underside, which is lacquered black,
has been impressed with an earth diaper while still soft.
Is this from the Ryukyu Islands?

It would be strange if there had been no attempt to
carve lacquer in Korea but neither carved nor pseudo-
carved lacquers from that country have yet been identified. Plain Korean lacquer is rare but is recognisable by
its distinctive light orange-red colour and by the way
that corners and edges are secured with small bronze
brackets. More typical Korean lacquer is inlaid with
mother-of-pearl, a technique derived from the Tang
that became so well-established in Korea that there was
little incentive to absorb and develop any later imported style. Once again the familiar difficulty arises: if
the Koreans did to some extent experiment with carved
lacquer would their work not almost certainly have become lost in the great body of Chinese lacquer and be
no longer distinguishable? Or would we be able to de-
tect something of the soft, subtle, modest, amateurish
quality that marks Korean ceramics?

There is as yet no evidence that other South East Asian
lands — Burma, Vietnam, Indonesia — who developed
their own way of using lacquer, owed anything directly
to China. The theory that Burma acquired the art from
Yunnan, though probable enough, is unsupported.

Not much is known of these peripheral lacquers; it may
be that there is not much to know. Although such
pieces may, when identified, turn out to be unexciting,
collectors and students should be alert to the possibility
that some of the more unusual pieces of carved lacquer
they come across were not made in China. They should
not be spurned for that reason. The ripples that reach
the edge of a pond have their own interest.

APPENDIX: CARVED LACQUER ARTISTS

Lee Yu-kuan (1972) lists some thirty lacquer artists of the Yuan, Ming and Qing dynasties; most are shadowy figures referred to in the literature whose work has not been identified. Of these, some are recorded only as having worked in other lacquer techniques such as inlaying with mother of pearl. Of those who are known to have been lacquer carvers, the most famous are ZHANG CHENG and YANG MAO who, according to the *Ge Gu Yao Lun* (David, 1971), came from Yanghui in Xietang (Jiashan, prefecture of Jiaxing, Zhejiang province). It was formerly thought that Yanghui, rather than being the name of a place, was the name of their master, but Garner (1979) was convinced this was not so. A number of pieces ostensibly signed by one or other of these two Yuan lacquerers are known, but because the reference to them was widely known it has been thought likely that many of these are forgeries. However, as the signatures almost invariably appear on pieces that *might* have been made by them, it would be well to suspend disbelief unless there are indications to the contrary. It seems reasonable to accept that signed pieces in the Palace Collection in Beijing are genuine. The leys jar *(Pl. 18)* and the octagonal dish *(Pl. 31)* are signed by Yang Mao; and a dish *(Pl. 23)* is signed by Zhang Cheng, as is the six lobed dish show by Bluett and Sons (Krahl and Morgan, 1989: Pl. 31). Another Yuan dish in Beijing (Palace Museum, 1985: Pl. 5) is signed by ZHANG MINDE about whom nothing further appears to be known. It is recorded that the Yongle Emperor, having sent for the two famous lacquer masters, learned that they were dead and appointed instead the son of Zhang Cheng, ZHANG DEGANG, to be assistant director in charge of lacquer production. His work has not been identified. Rather more is known of the career of YANG XUAN (*fl.* 1426–64) whose father, otherwise unknown, was also a lacquerer. During the reign of Zhengtong, Yang Xuan worked as a lacquerer in Beijing, but was caught up in Court politics and achieved fame as a victim of injustice. his name is associated with the Japanese technique of using gold and silver on lacquer and it is doubtful if he was a lacquer carver (Goodrich, 1976).

Better authenticated is WANG MING from the village of Pingliang in Gansu province who signed the famous dish in the British Museum *(Pl. 58)* which is dated 1489. A box in the Freer gallery of Art *(Pl. 59)* bears a similar inscription, and a screen in the Tokyo National Museum is signed by 'WANG YAN of Pingliang', supposed to be the brother of Wang Ming.

A Ming lacquerer whose work has been identified by one example is WU BAOSU who signed the leys jar in plate 69. he appears to be the same person as an ink-maker of the well-known Wu family of ink-makers (Moss, 1986). The style of this jar is compatible with an early Jiajing date.

HUANG CHENG (*fl.* 1567–72), who complied an *Account of the Decoration of Lacquer* in the late sixteenth century, was said to be a famous lacquerer whose work was already being copied in 1591. A preface to his book was written in 1625 by YANG MING, himself a lacquerer. No examples by these two artists are known. Another lacquerer whose work one would wish to see was the TIANQI EMPEROR (reigned 1621–27).

The work of two Qing lacquerers has been identified. LU GUISHENG (Li, 1957) signed four panels (illustrated in Moss, 1983) of which one is shown in plate 117. His dates are uncertain but 1780–1850 is suggested. The majority of his known work dates from the beginning of Daoguang, but some pieces bear Qianlong reign marks. SUN GUOXIN *(Pl. 118)* was clearly an associate. In some ways his 'Landscape with Lutanist' is more strikingly individual.

Lee Yu-kuan (1972, pp. 169–70) refers to LAO WEI and ZHANG GUI as lacquerers working at the beginning of the twentieth century, but it does not appear that they worked in carved lacquer. Lee also mentions ZHEN RIZHU who made a large red carved lacquer food box for the Dowager Empress Cixi. He is said to have run a lacquer factory and Lee reports that his work was definitely 'more beautiful and stronger' than that made in the reign of Daoguang. Unfortunately, he illustrated no work by Zhen Rizhu and none has been recorded.

SELECT BIBLIOGRAPHY

Arts Council, 1957 *Arts of the Ming Dynasty*, London.

Asian Art Museum of San Francisco, 1986 *Marvels of Medieval China*, San Francisco.

Ayers, J. G., 1974 'A Carved Red Lacquer Table', in *Furniture History*, Furniture History Society, London.

Boston Museum of Fine Arts, 1982 *Asiatic Art in the Museum of Fine Arts, Boston*.

Brandt, Klaus Joachim, 1988 *Chinesische Lackarbeiten*, Linden-Museum, Stuttgart. A thoroughly researched catalogue of an important collection.

Budapest Museum of Applied Arts, 1981 *Oriental Lacquer Work*, Budapest. Catalogue of an exhibition in the Castle Museum of Nagytetemy from the collection of the Ferenc Hopp Museum of Asiatic Art.

Burmeister, A., 1988 'Technical Studies of Chinese Lacquer' in Urushi: *Proceedings of the 1985 Urushi Study Group*, Marina del Rey, California.

Champkins, Paul, 1983 *The Minor Arts of China*, Spink & Son Ltd, London.

Chen Jing, 1979 'Important Southern Song Lacquers Newly Excavated at Wujin, Jiangsu', *Wenwu* no. 3, Wenwu Press, Beijing.

Clunas, Craig, 1991 'Whose Throne is it Anyway? The Qianlong Throne in the T. T. Tsui Gallery', in *Orientations*, Hong Kong, July issue.

David, Sir Percival, 1971 *Chinese Connoisseurship, The Ko Ku Yao Lun*, Faber & Faber, London.

Feng Han-chi, 1961 'P'ing-t'o Lacquer and Silver Inlaid Lacquer Excavated from the Tomb of Wang Chien of Former Shu', *Wenwu* no. 11, Wenwu Press, Beijing.

Figgess, John, 1962–63 'A Letter from the Court of Yung-lo', *Transactions of the Oriental Ceramic Society* vol. 34, London.

Figgess, John, 1967–69 'Ming and Pre-Ming Lacquer in the Japanese Tea Ceremony', *Transactions of the Oriental Ceramic Society* vol. 37, London. A most important contribution to the understanding of Chinese lacquer from the Japanese point of view.

Gabbert, Gunhild, 1978. *Ostasiatische Lackkunst*, Museum für Kunsthandwerk, Frankfurt am Main.

Garner, Harry M., 1957–59 'Guri Lacquer of the Ming Dynasty', *Transactions of the Oriental Ceramic Society* vol. 31, London.

Garner, Harry M., 1960 *Ming Lacquer:* An Exhibition arranged by Bluett & Sons, London.

Garner, Harry M., 1966 'Diaper Backgrounds on Chinese Carved Lacquer', *Ars Orientalis* vol. 6, New York and Tokyo. The most important of Garner's scholarly contributions.

Garner, Harry M., 1966–67 'A Group of Chinese Lacquers with Basketry Panels', *Archives of Asian Art* vol. 20, New York.

Garner, Harry M., 1972 'The Export of Chinese Lacquer to Japan in the Yuan and Early Ming Dynasties', *Archives of Asian Art* vol. 25, New York.

Garner, Harry M., 1973a 'Two Chinese Carved Lacquer Boxes of the Fifteenth Century in the Freer Gallery of Art', *Ars Orientalis* vol. 9, New York and Tokyo.

Garner, Harry M., 1973b *Chinese and Associated Lacquer from the Garner Collection*, British Museum, London.

Garner Harry M., 1979 *Chinese Lacquer*, Faber & Faber, London. Perhaps the most widely read study of the subject, rather conservative in approach.

Goodrich, L. Carrington, 1976 *Dictionary of Ming Biography 1368–1644*, Columbia University Press, New York and London. Of great value for understanding the Ming background.

Helen Foresman Spencer Museum of Art, University of Kansas, 1980 *Catalogue of the Oriental Collection*.

Herberts, K. 1963 *Oriental Lacquer*, New York. (First publication in German, Dusseldorf, 1959)

Impey, O. R. and Tregear, M., 1983 *Chinese and Japanese Lacquer from the Ashmolean Collection*, Ashmolean Museum, Oxford.

Itabashi Ward Museum, 1983 *Exhibition of Lacquerware from the Ryukyu Islands: Mikokai Collection*, Tokyo.

Jenyns, R. Soames, 1939–40 'Chinese Lacquer', *Transactions of the Oriental Ceramic Society* vol. 17, London.

Jenyns, R. Soames and Watson, William, 1963 *Chinese Art: The Minor Arts*, London.

Jourdain, M. and Jenyns, R. Soames, 1950 *Chinese Export Art*, London.

Krahl, Regina and Morgan, Brian, 1989 *From Innovation to Conformity*, Bluett & Sons Ltd, London. The catalogue of an exhibition of the finest collection ever offered for sale.

Kuwayama, George, 1982 *Far Eastern Lacquer: An Exhibition Catalogue of the Los Angeles County Museum of Art's Permanent Collection*, Los Angeles. The introduction contains an admirable brief history of Chinese lacquer.

Kuwayama, George, 1988 'Chinese Guri Lacquers' in Urushi: *Proceedings of the Urushi Study Group*, Marina del Rey.

Lee King Tsi, 1990 *Dragon and Phoenix: Chinese Lacquer, The Lee Family Collection*, Museum für Ostasiatische Kunst, Köln.

Lee Yu-kuan, 1964 *Chinese Lacquer as Exhibited at the Royal Scottish Museum*, Edinburgh.

Lee Yu-kuan, 1972 *Oriental Lacquer Art*, Weatherhill, New York and Tokyo. An important quarry of information which is sometimes inaccurate and often difficult to disentangle because of poor arrangement. It is a valuable counter-agent to the conservative views of Garner.

Li Hongqing, 1957 'The Lacquer of the Ming and the Ch'ing, and the Carved Lacquer of the Yuan', *Wenwu* no. 7, Wenwu Press, Beijing.

Low Beer, F., 1950 'Chinese Lacquer of the Early Fifteenth Century', *Bulletin of the Museum of Far Eastern Antiquities* no. 22, Stockholm. This, with his later study of 'Chinese Lacquer of the Middle and Late Ming Periods', was a most important early contribution.

Low Beer, F., 1952 'Chinese Lacquer of the Middle and Late Ming Periods', *Bulletin of the Museum of Far Eastern Antiquities* no. 24, Stockholm.

Low Beer, F., 1977 'Carved Lacquer of the Yuan Dynasty: A Re-assessment', *Oriental Art* vol. 23 no. 3, Richmond, Surrey. This challenges some of Garner's attributions of certain Yuan bird-and-flower dishes. It has not met with general acceptance.

Luzzatto-Blitz, Oscar, 1984. *Lacche Orientali*, Fabbri Editori, Milan.

Moss, Paul, 1983 *Documentary Chinese Works of Art: In Scholars' Taste*, Sydney L. Moss Ltd, London.

Moss, Paul, 1986 *The Literati Mode*, Sydney L. Moss Ltd, London.

Nara National Museum 1982 *Flowers of Buddhist Applied Art*.

National Art Treasures of Korea, 1961, The Arts Council, Seoul.

National Museum of Korea, 1977 *Sinan Yonan Munmul* (Cultural Relics Found off the Sinan Coast), Samhwa Publishing Co., Seoul. Exhibition catalogue.

National Palace Museum, Taiwan, 1971 *Masterpieces of Chinese Carved Lacquerware in the National Palace Museum*, Taibei.

National Palace Museum, Taiwan, 1981 *Catalogue of Chinese Lacquer*, Taibei.

National Palace Museum, Taiwan, 1987 *Chinese Art in Overseas Collections: Lacquerware*, Taibei. A valuable collection of illustrations of which only a few are captioned in English.

Okada Jo, 1969 *So no Tsuishu* (Chinese Carved Lacquer of the Song Dynasty), Tokyo National Museum, Tokyo.

Okada Jo, 1977 *Oriental Lacquer Art*, Tokyo National Museum, Tokyo. Exhibition catalogue with an important assembly of illustrations. This publication is not easily obtainable.

Palace Museum, 1985 *Carved Lacquer in the Collection of the Palace Museum*, Gugong Bowuyuan, Beijing. A magnificent assemblage of illustrations of the Beijing Palace Collection. The black-and-white reproductions are of poor quality.

Ráth György Museum, 1987 *Chinese Arts*, Budapest.

Riddell, Sheila 1979 *Dated Chinese Antiquities 600–1650*, Faber & Faber, London.

Rijksmuseum, Amsterdam, 1978–79 *Vereniging Van Vrieden der Aziatische Kunst*.

Scott, Rosemary *et al.*, 1984 *Lacquer: An International History and Collector's Guide*, Crowood Press/Phoebe Phillips Editions, Marlborough.

Shi Shujing, 1957 'A Sung Carved Lacquer Box of the Zhenghe Period', *Wenwu* no. 7, Wenwu Press, Beijing.

Smithsonian Institute, 1987 *Asian Art in the Arthur M. Sackler Gallery,* Washington.

Spence, Jonathan D., 1984 *The Memory Palace of Matteo Ricci,* Faber & Faber, London.

Spink & Son Ltd., 1983 *See* Champkins above.

Spink & Son Ltd., 1987 *The Minor Arts of China III,* London.

Spink & Son Ltd., 1988 *Octagon,* vol. xxv, no. 1, London.

Spink & Son Ltd., 1989 *The Minor Arts of China IV,* London.

Spink & Son Ltd., 1991 *Chinese Art at Spink,* London.

Strange, E. F., 1925 *Catalogue of Chinese Lacquer in the Victoria and Albert Museum,* Her Majesty's Stationery Office, London.

Strange, E. F., 1926. *Chinese Lacquer,* Ernest Benn, London. This contains some good illustrations although from limited and now familiar sources. A more useful introductory book than the savage notice in the *Times Literary Supplement* of 1926 would have one believe.

Strasser, Edith, 1988 *Ex Oriente Lux: Oriental and European Lacquer from the BASF Lacquer Museum, Köln.*

Tokyo National Museum, 1974. *Ch'iang-Chin* [Qiangjin], *Chinkin and Zonsei Lacquerware,* Tokyo.

Tokyo National Museum, 1977. *Oriental Lacquer Arts,* Tokyo.

Tokyo National Museum, 1989 *Art of the Muromachi Period,* Tokyo. Special exhibition catalogue.

Tsung Tien, 1959 'Yuan Ren Renfa muzhi faxian' ('The Discovery of the Yuan Ren Renfa's Tomb Remains'), *Wenwu* no. 11, Wenwu Press, Beijing.

Vanderhoef Sr., F. Bailey, 1976 *Oriental Lacquer,* Santa Barbara Museum of Art, Santa Barbara. Exhibition catalogue.

Wang Shixiang, 1987 *Ancient Chinese Lacquerware,* Foreign Languages Press, Beijing. The most luxurious of modern publications by a great Chinese authority.

Watson, William (ed.), 1981 'Lacquerwork in Asia and Beyond', *Colloquies on Art and Archaeology in Asia* no. 11, Percival David Foundation, London.

Watt, James, 1991 *East Asian Lacquer: The Florence and Herbert Irving Collection,* The Metropolitan Museum of Art, New York.

Wirgin, Jan, 1966 'An Early Fifteenth Century Lacquer Box', *Bulletin of the Museum of Far Eastern Antiquities* no. 38, Stockholm.

Wirgin, Jan, 1972 'Some Chinese Carved Lacquer of the Yuan and Ming Periods', *Bulletin of the Museum of Far Eastern Antiquities* no. 44, Stockholm.

Winkworth, W. W. *et al.,* 1935 *Chinese Art,* Batsford, London.

Zhu Jiajin, 1988 Article in *Orientations,* Hong Kong, March issue.